COVENANT • BIBLE • STUDIES

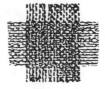

Uncovering Racism

Kathryn Goering Reid
Stephen Breck Reid

faithQuest® ◆ Brethren Press®

Covenant Bible Studies Series

Cover photo: D. Jeanene Tiner

03   02   01   00   99   5   4   3   2   1

Library of Congress Cataloging in Publication Data
Reid, Kathryn Goering.
    Uncovering racism / Kathryn Goering Reid, Stephen Breck Reid.
       p.   cm. -- (Covenant Bible studies)
       Includes bibliographical references.
    ISBN 0-87178-016-X (alk. paper)
          1. Race relations--Biblical teaching.   2. Racism--Religious aspects--
          Christianity.   3. Bible--Study and teaching.   I. Reid, Stephen Breck.
          II. Title.   III. Series: Covenant Bible study series.
    BS680.R2R45 1999
    261.8'348--dc21   99-23619

Manufactured in the United States of America

Contents

For further reading:

America's Original Sin: A Study Guide on White Racism. Sojourn-ers magazine, 1992.

Ball, Edward. *Slaves in the Family.* Ballantine Books, 1998, 1999.

Bell, Derrick A. *Faces from the Bottom of the Well: The Permanence of Racism in America.* Basic, 1993.

Carnes, Jim. *Us and Them: A History of Intolerance in America* (Video and Study Guide). Southern Poverty Law Center, 1995.

Carter, Forrest. *The Education of Little Tree.* University of New Mexico Press, 1976.

Houston, Jeanne W. and James D. Houston. *Farewell to Manzanar,* Bantam, 1983.

"Intelligence Project." Southern Poverty Law Center, 400 Washington Ave., Montgomery, AL 36104. www.splcenter.org/intelligenceproject.

Morrison, Toni. *Beloved.* Penguin, 1987.

Williams, Gregory Howard. *Life on the Color Line.* Penguin Group, 1995.

Foreword

The Covenant Bible Studies Series was first developed for a denominational program in the Church of the Brethren and the Christian Church (Disciples of Christ). This program, called People of the Covenant, was founded on the concept of relational Bible study and has been adopted by several other denominations and small groups who want to study the Bible in a community rather than alone.

Relational Bible study is marked by certain characteristics, some of which differ from other types of Bible study. For one, it is intended for small groups of people who can meet face-to-face on a regular basis and share frankly with an intimate group.

It is important to remember that relational Bible study is anchored in covenantal history. God covenanted with people in Old Testament history, established a new covenant in Jesus Christ, and covenants with the church today.

Relational Bible study takes seriously a corporate faith. As each person contributes to study, prayer, and work, the group becomes the real body of Christ. Each one's contribution is needed and important. "For just as the body is one and has many members, and all the members of the body, though many, are one body, so it is with Christ. . . . Now you are the body of Christ and individually members of it" (1 Cor. 12:12, 17).

Relational Bible study helps both individuals and the group to claim the promise of the Spirit and the working of the Spirit. As one person testified, "In our commitment to one another and in our sharing, something happened. . . . We were woven together in love by the Master Weaver. It is something that can happen only when two or three or seven are gathered in God's name, and we know the promise of God's presence in our lives."

The symbol for these covenant Bible study groups is the burlap cross. The interwoven threads, the uniqueness of each strand, the unrefined fabric, and the rough texture characterize covenant groups. The people in the groups are unique but interrelated; they are imperfect and unpolished, but loving and supportive.

The shape that these divergent threads create is the cross, the symbol for all Christians of the resurrection and presence with us of Christ our Savior. Like the burlap cross, we are brought together, simple and ordinary, to be sent out again in all directions to be in the world.

For people who choose to use this study in a small group, the following guidelines will help create an atmosphere in which support will grow and faith will deepen.

1. As a small group of learners, we gather around God's word to discern its meaning for today.
2. The words, stories, and admonitions we find in scripture come alive for today, challenging and renewing us.
3. All people are learners and all are leaders.
4. Each person will contribute to the study, sharing the meaning found in the scripture and helping to bring meaning to others.
5. We recognize each other's vulnerability as we share out of our own experience, and in sharing we learn to trust others and to be trustworthy.

Additional suggestions for study and group-building are provided in the "Sharing and Prayer" section. They are intended for use in the hour preceding the Bible study to foster intimacy in the covenant group and relate personal sharing to the Bible study topic.

Welcome to this study. As you search the scriptures, may you also search yourself. May God's voice and guidance and the love and encouragement of brothers and sisters in Christ challenge you to live more fully the abundant life God promises.

Preface

I grew up in a small, all white, Midwestern college town whose blend of intellectuals, local merchants, laborers, and philosopher farmers made for a progressive upbringing. Martin Luther King, Jr., came to town to speak at the college just a month before he was assassinated. Paul Newman campaigned here for presidential primary candidate Robert Kennedy. My draft-age brother did not register and attended one of the moratoria on the war in Washington, D.C. Everyone I knew was loving and open and indignant about injustice. It was a rare and stimulating childhood.

I don't know when it came to my consciousness that for all our open-mindedness we had no experience living with people of other races. Maybe it was when we trooped off with my parents to see the then shocking film *Guess Who's Coming to Dinner* about a young white woman who brings her black fiancé home to meet her parents. Maybe it was the time I was shopping with my mother in her hometown when a caravan of Klansmen pulled up and began parading around the courthouse square. She recalled at that moment the awful incident of her childhood in which a black man was lynched on that very courthouse lawn. Maybe it was a Council of Churches youth project to play with the children of Mexican migrant workers. Maybe it was a trip with the youth group to visit "Operation Breadbasket" in Chicago, the Southern Christian Leadership Conference (SCLC) project to promote jobs and equality for people of color. Senator Percy of Illinois spoke to a huge crowd that day, Jesse Jackson presided as the staff person, and Aretha Franklin sang in a style I'd never dreamed of before.

My heart was in the right place, but all my experience was secondhand. Finally, I was rescued from my provincialism by Steve Reid and Kathy Goering, a dating couple in college who volunteered to lead the youth group at my church. Steve was

African American and Kathy white. Of all the things I remember about my personal education in race relations in those days, the one that shook me up was an offhand comment Steve made one day to the group. We must have been talking about jogging or something equally banal when Steve said he could never run down the street in this small town. Whoever sees a black man running, he said, will assume he is running from something, vandalism, theft, or rape.

I didn't want to think that was true in my ideal little world, but the prejudices Steve and Kathy experienced, and to which we youth were privy, proved Steve was right. Ever after, I could see the roots of racism growing deep into the community, touching everything. A black couple associated with the college had trouble buying a house. A visiting Ecuadoran man was picked up by police who assumed he was where he shouldn't be. A white high school student posted an anonymous threat in the locker of one of only several black students at the high school. People of color who told about brush-offs from whites were considered "overly sensitive."

Why do I continue to live here in the midst of racism? Maybe it's the same inertia that keeps privileged whites from really challenging racism. I don't know for sure. For one thing my family is here. And besides, there is not a place to go where racism is not. The advantage of my inertia is that it leaves me living among the people I know best and among whom I may have the greatest influence. But no matter where we are, whether we're among the familiar or the unfamiliar, we are among fellow human beings, created in the image of God. Wherever we are, we can defend the God-given value of every individual, dispel unfair prejudices, and decry racism. It doesn't so much matter where we live as how we live. It matters most that we can say we have lived "to the glory of God and my neighbor's good."

–Julie Garber
1999

1

Challenged by a Dream
Acts 10

Racial minorities in the U.S. are growing and blending at such a fast rate that statisticians say the United States will be less than half white by 2050. Yet there is perhaps more racism and intolerance today than ever before. Sadly, churches are part of these trends. This study works at educating Christians about racism and encourages them to work against it and for the world that God intended.

Personal Preparation

1. Read Acts 10, Peter's dream. Also, read, listen to, or recall Martin Luther King, Jr.'s "I have a dream" speech. In what ways are these dreams alike? How would you express your dream for God's people?

2. Put yourself in Peter's sandals. What would you do if you had to choose between obeying the commands of the Bible or obeying what seemed like the voice of God in a dream, especially if the two commands conflicted? Why?

3. Why do you think God would say something different to Peter than was said in the Holy Scriptures? Have you ever felt that God is saying a new thing today? What is it?

4. Sing or read the spiritual hymn "Let my people go." This spiritual expresses the feelings of the children of Israel as they faced Pharaoh in Egypt. It also expresses

the feelings of African slaves trapped in slavery in the United States. Of course, the universal theme of being enslaved in sin is a theme with which all people can empathize. In what ways are you enslaved in your life?

Understanding

A community on the East Coast recently dealt with a racist and hateful act when a group of unknown teenagers trashed and destroyed a Jewish family's menorah at Christmas time. The shocked and embarrassed community responded by asking Christian families to show their support of the Jewish family by putting menorahs on their Christmas trees. The Jewish family was pleasantly surprised by the love and care shown by the Christian community. Unfortunately, the experience of racism and discrimination is often not addressed so directly and clearly.

Nearly thirty years ago, Dr. Martin Luther King, Jr., led a movement of people, including religious people, against the ugly reality of racial discrimination and racism in the United States. Many of the overt examples of discrimination ended. "Whites Only" drinking fountains, restaurants, and motels were eliminated. Segregated buses and trains became integrated. Equal opportunity slogans became popular in businesses. The Ku Klux Klan seemed to be losing power.

However, just when we think equal opportunity is the order of the day, we are reminded that perhaps things are not as good as they seem. Public scandals at the highest levels of large corporations remind us that job discrimination is all too common. Cross-burnings and Klan marches continue with little publicity. Perhaps the greatest embarrassment for people of faith is that the Sunday church hour is the most segregated hour of the week. Few churches are inclusive of people of different races, and even ethnic churches seldom cooperate.

Unfortunately, racism is common around the world. North America is not the only continent that has a history of racial conflict and racism. Nevertheless, the history of the United States is shaped around attitudes of race. The slave trade touched the lives of not only those Africans kidnaped from their homes in Africa, but also the privileged white society that depended on the cheap labor of Africans. The abolitionist movement and religious support of the southern slave system divided many Protestant denominations. Naturally, the Civil War affected every aspect of American life in the nineteenth century. More recently, the civil rights movement spread the ideas of equality and began the antiracist movement. Presently, discussions about race are often mixed with discussion of immigration and preferential hiring.

Racial conflicts in this country have not been limited to black/white issues. There is a commonality of experience of racism among people of color. Sometimes the racism is based on skin color, but there can be other components of culture, language, and legal status. As a matter of fact, racism involving other cultures and ethnic groups is growing as those groups grow. By the year 2050 the American population will be 32 percent Asian/Pacific American, Latino, and Native American.

Racism involving specific groups is often more obvious in specific areas or regions. Throughout the country, Native American people were removed from their homelands and sent to reservations. Racial and cultural conflicts still exist in places where native people encounter people of European descent. Historically, the southern part of the United States has been a place of overt racism against African Americans. However, many people would agree that racial conflict between African Americans and white Americans exists throughout the country. In the Southwest, Hispanic people have experienced prejudice. Even between minority groups there are racial conflicts. Asian Americans and African Americans have a history of racial conflict. Perhaps you can think of others.

For centuries researchers have wondered whether prejudice is a natural human condition. However, when researchers observe small children, they see that children may be curious about differences, but they easily make friendships that cross racial lines and are not racist. This observation leads many people to believe that racism and prejudice are attitudes transmitted from one generation to another. In other words, our children learn from our words and actions about how to treat people of different races.

Prejudice is defined as a preference for one kind of person over another. Stereotyping is an important aspect of prejudice, because generally we make judgments about an individual based on generalizations about an entire category of people. For example, the following are common stereotypes: African Americans are great basketball players; only white football players are good quarterbacks; German Americans are hardworking, industrious people; Scottish people are very frugal. You can add to this list.

Discrimination is an action against one person and in favor of another because of race or ethnic background. Unfortunately, it is all too common for corporations and even small businesses to still have an unwritten, unspoken policy either to not hire a particular minority or to not promote those people despite their skills and abilities. All too often minority people are discriminated against.

It is important to know that racism is not only a bias against a person because of their skin color or ethnic background, but it also includes the power to act on that bias. For example, an individual may be prejudiced against Hispanics, but he or she is, in fact, racist when he or she gives Hispanic workers lower annual job performance ratings, resulting in fewer promotions. It is more than just prejudice when one has the power to act on his or her preferences of one race over another.

Antiracism is an active personal, professional, and corporate attitude that works against racism. A person who is not racist may quietly listen to a racist joke. However, an antiracist person makes an issue of the offensive nature of the joke. A company or religious institution that is antiracist has policies and procedures in place that make it clear that racist attitudes will not be tolerated and that all employees and supervisors will be actively working against prejudice and racism.

In the New Testament, Acts 10 describes a profound and life-changing experience for Peter. He encounters a divine vision that is mysterious to him and also to us and unlike any other vision described in the Bible. The text does not explain the role of the unclean animals and the great sheets of sailcloth. There is no interpretation of the vision included in the text.

Nevertheless, the impact on Peter is clear. Peter is horrified and repulsed by the idea of violating the Jewish food laws. Yet, he is challenged by the perplexity and mystery of the vision's meaning. Peter has no doubt that this mysterious, divine revelation is leading him. The truth of the vision paves the way for Peter to meet Cornelius and to become Christ's witness to the Gentiles.

Peter's sermon found in 10:34-43 makes an important statement about God's intention to include all people. "Then Peter began to speak to them: 'I truly understand that God shows no partiality, but in every nation anyone who fears him and does what is right is acceptable to him' " (Acts 10:34). Peter centers his sermon on God's nature and what God has done through Christ. Peter emphasizes to the Gentiles the continuing stories of God's saving acts.

The events recounted in Acts were crucial turning points in the spreading of the story of Jesus Christ and God's love for the world. Although Peter's sermon is not unique, the distinctive element is Peter's insistence that God does not "play favorites." In Christ, all are able to realize God's intended vision of an interracial humanity. God fully accepts all people, Jews and Gentiles. The old categories and barriers between people no longer exist. Even the rules about "unclean" and "clean" have fallen away. Just as God accepts all people, we as members of the interracial family of God are called to accept each other. If Peter had any questions about God's acceptance of the Gentiles, it seems that his vision has propelled him into a ministry that reaches out to all people. Difference should not be an excuse for the exercise of racial privilege.

Martin Luther King, Jr. shared Peter's vision of an interracial family of God. Christians around the world are challenged by these dreams to be antiracist. The civil rights movement of the 1960s and the ending of apartheid in South Africa are both good examples that racism and discrimination do not simply die out, but it takes the actions and words of people of faith to change the attitudes and actions of those around us.

All too often in our small quiet communities we forget about the ongoing evil of racism in our world until some incident or action reminds us that racism is alive and well all around us. Peter was challenged to take the good news of the gospel to the Gentiles. He crossed the boundary of his own ethnic and racial group. Like Peter, we are challenged to tell others and to take actions to bring together the interracial family of God.

Discussion and Action

1. On newsprint, list common racial stereotypes for African Americans, Asians, Hispanics, Native Americans, and people of European descent. Use descriptive words such as stupid, smart, colorful, lazy, militant, overly sensitive, arrogant, rigid, controlling, sneaky, loud, and any others you can think of. Review the lists. Are the stereotypical words positive or negative in each category? How do you think groups of people got these stereotypes?

2. Take a minute to personally list ways you think race relations have improved since the civil rights movement of the 1960s. Then list ways that you think race relations have gotten worse since the sixties. Share your lists with each other. In general, are things better or worse? Why?

3. What stories do you remember hearing from your parents and grandparents about racial conflict in the past? Looking back, did the stories stereotype parties in the conflict? In what ways?

4. How have you tried to teach your children about race equality? How successful do you think you've been?

5. What books have you read recently that show some aspect of racism? Can you think of a movie or television program whose theme is racism and prejudice? How effective are books, television, and movies in overcoming racism? How do these media reinforce racial stereotypes?

6. Where in your community do you see racial tensions? If you live in a community or neighborhood that is made up of people of only one race, why is that so? Why would

people of other races be afraid to live in your community? Why would you or would you not want to live in a mixed race neighborhood?

7. In preparation for this lesson, each participant was asked to dream of what the world would look like if we lived as God wishes. Share your dreams with each other. How does God truly want people to live together? How much like Peter's or King's dream is your dream? How is it different?

8. Mention some of your own prejudices. In what ways have you ever discriminated based on racial prejudice? In what ways have you ever been discriminated against? Have you yourself or anyone you know ever used his or her authority or position to discriminate against a person of a different race? If you can, tell the group about it.

9. Sing together "Let my people go."

2

The Power That Oppresses
Matthew 18:23-35

Racism is more than simple prejudice. It is prejudice with the power to affect another's life. Throughout history, people have had power over others. Even biblical history is filled with power struggles between people and nations, but Jesus taught the disciples about the dangers of power when it's in the hands of too few. In order to end racism, people must share power.

Personal Preparation

1. Read Matthew 18:23-35. How is power used in the parable to harm others? How is it used for good? How much power do you have in your life? parental? financial? managerial? educational? racial? How can you be sure that you are using it all for good?

2. Look closely at the biblical timeline on pages 98-102 that illustrates the power and control people of the Bible had over each other. Notice that those who were slaves later enslaved others. If you suddenly had power, how would you use it?

3. Read Psalm 4:2-3. The psalmist laments the people's attacks on God's honor but at the same time notes that God hears and cares about the situation of human suffering. How does God's endless grace affect the way you treat others?

4. Read the words to "Lift every voice and sing."

Understanding

An historical examination of the term *racism* might be helpful. It comes from the word *racial*, meaning "with regard to race." During the nineteenth and early twentieth centuries, racism was seen differently than today. Racism was the prejudice based on race. In that era, people who were racist overtly treated people of color with contempt. But often those who claimed not to be racist were still vocal in the preference for European tradition. In other words, people were not judged racist even if they thought that all white people were superior and that non-European cultures were primitive. Racism was thought to be more indicative of behavior, not attitude.

For example, there were many abolitionists who were very proud that they treated slaves and former slaves politely. At the same time, they still believed in superiority of the white race and did not want to have any contact with people of color. Today we judge someone as prejudiced or racist by his or her attitudes and actions. However, there are members of an older generation who still do not view themselves as racist because they treat people of color politely—all the while holding what others might call racist attitudes.

As the racial tyranny of the nineteenth and early twentieth centuries gave way to more subtle forms of social control, most white Americans assumed that given a choice all people would choose to be white. European Americans were shocked that there could be ethnic groups who were proud of their own ethnic and cultural heritage. At that point many European Americans were offended by what they perceived as the "racism" of "those groups."

As white Americans watched the pride and power movements of some ethnic groups emerge and also perhaps the emergence of prejudice of nonwhite individuals, the definition of racism shifted. The European American argued that all but the most vicious and violent of "white racism" was justified because victims of white racism had their individual prejudices, too. Either "everyone is racist, so don't bother me," or "take the racism out of your own community before you confront me about the racism in mine."

Particularly after the civil rights movement in the 1950s, '60s and '70s, the European American community had tired of struggling with race.

The designation "racism" has become more vague these days. Racism is prejudice based on race plus the power to implement those prejudices to the detriment of another. Our friend Iris speaks perfect English. If you talked to her on the phone, you would never know that not only is she Hispanic, but at one time Spanish was her only language. That was before she started school. At her parochial school, the Catholic sisters did not approve of anything of Mexican culture. Iris was not allowed to speak Spanish in school, not even during recess on the playground. The punishment was a spanking. For years, she was sent from the classroom to a speech therapist to "correct" her accent.

Not only did Iris lose much of her Spanish language, but she was successful in losing her accent. What other aspects of her native Mexican culture did she lose because the Catholic sisters did not approve of her culture? What happened to her self-esteem as she was forced to see herself as a "dirty Mexican"? Not only were the Catholic sisters prejudiced against Hispanic people, but they had the power to force compliance with their ideas of cultural superiority. The school's power and prejudice resulted in a racist system that oppressed minority children.

Power and Racism in the Church

When the church does not pay attention to power, the church subverts its own attempts to come to terms with the sin of racism. One type of such sabotage involves the claim that there is no place in Christianity for power. Rather than recognize the power that each of us has in our jobs, our homes, and within our church, we sometimes claim that Christians have no power.

In the biblical text, we find a distinction between the history of oppression and that of power. Deuteronomy tells us, "You shall love the Lord your God with all your heart, and with all your soul, and with all your might" (6:5). The Hebrew for *power* is translated as might and is used in a positive sense. It is a power that builds up, a power that glorifies God. Similarly, the Greek word for power also occurs numerous times in the Bible. But the New Testament understands that power also possesses a demonic side as well as a good side. When power is demonic it is used to oppress. The Letter to the Ephesians reminds us that when we battle racism we are not contending with flesh and blood but against principalities and powers (6:12a). Racism— that is, prejudice with power—is nothing less than a demonic power. It calls for a righteous use of power to counter it.

Jesus taught his disciples about the use of power in Matthew 18:23-35, the story of the unforgiving servant. The kingdom of God is compared to a king who wants to settle all his accounts with his slaves. One slave owes so much that the king declares that he should be sold along with his wife, children, and all his property. The slave begs the king for forgiveness. The king uses his power for good as he forgives the slave. But the slave, who has power over another who owes him, chooses to use his power cruelly by throwing this slave into prison.

For generations, people have been perplexed by the fact that sometimes those who are oppressed turn into oppressors of others when they get a little power. Sometimes different racial groups, all of whom experience discrimination and hatred, cannot get along together. Rather than learning to be compassionate and caring from the experience of oppression, some use whatever power they have to oppress others and escape their own oppression.

When our family lived in Fiji, our children's darker skin and curly hair fit well into the natural skin tones and racial characteristics of native Fijians. The purpose of our trip was to visit a Pacific culture while Steve taught at the seminary in Suva. Steve organized his biblical theology class to include liberation theology. However, the native Fijians could not understand a theology that stands with the oppressed. The Fijian students of Indian descent, however, were completely fascinated by this new approach to biblical studies. The Indian population was brought to the islands by the British to work the plantations and provide the labor for the island. The descendants of those servants and poor laborers have now become the merchants and much of the educated class of the society. They are still the oppressed of the island, however. Not long after we left the island, a political coup overthrew the democratic government, which included Indian leaders. The result of the coup was that the Indian population lost most of their rights and many Indian people left the island.

Steve found himself physically looking like the native Fijian students all the while relating to the Indian students who had experienced a discrimination similar to African Americans in the United States. The Indian students read their Bibles with new eyes when Steve taught them about the slavery of the Hebrew children and their exodus to freedom.

In the United States, people of European descent still control most of the industry and business in our society. People of color are generally more economically disadvantaged, less educated, and less able to move up the ladder of social status. Of course, there are exceptions. Some of those exceptions give us the illusion that racial equality is a reality. Sports stars, music celebrities, and other notable people give the impression that all people of color can attain wealth and notoriety. However, if a person looks at the statistics overall, it is clear that most people of color are not as advantaged as whites.

When you travel, note who cleans the room at the hotel, who serves the meal at the restaurant or fast food place, who carries luggage at the airport. Usually people of color work these lower paying jobs. Why does it seem that they cannot rise out of that station? Does a poorer educational system and a poorer upbringing keep them disadvantaged? A large part of the answer is that white privilege gives people of European descent an advantage. Those who have an advantage use their power to continue their control, sometimes unknowingly. Better jobs, quicker promotions, acceptance for home mortgages, and much more are the reality for those who experience white privilege. People of color, more often than not, experience discrimination, racism, and disadvantage.

Jesus reminds us that power does exist and as Christians we are called to use our power in a just and right manner. Respect for all people is part of being a Christian. As Christians we are called to be fair as bosses, as property owners, as people of power. We can use our power to make the world better. Like the king, we often have the power to do good.

Discussion and Action

1. Look at the biblical timeline together. This timeline shows how people and nations in Bible times exerted power over others. Overall, what impressions do you have of how God's people have used power? In what ways, if at all, have things changed? Where is power being used today to suppress people because of their race? To what extent is this happening in the United States?

2. What kinds of power do you have? How does power affect your relationships with others? How does power change relationships? Think of times when someone has gone from being a colleague to being a supervisor. Did personal relationships change?

3. What prejudices do you have? To what extent is everyone prejudiced? Does the prevalence of prejudice in our society give you a sense of urgency about combating prejudice or a sense of hopelessness that it can ever be eradicated? Why?

4. To what extent is it natural for people to have preferences for their friendships, their families, their neighbors, and others? How do these prejudices, even if they are natural, affect us personally? as a community? as the church?

5. Make two lists side-by-side. In the first list, name a few race prejudices that you talked about in question 3. In the second list, name a few ways in which you said you had power in question 2. Next, draw lines between your prejudices and the ways in which you have power to enforce your prejudices.

6. Think of a time when you encountered someone who was prejudiced against you because of race, money, education, gender, occupation, nationality, or any other reason. How did it make you feel? What did you say? How did it

affect your life? Did the prejudiced person have the power
to affect your job, your family, your life with his or her
own preferences? How? Was this a case of racism? How
did it fit the definition of racism used in this session?

7. Start a personal timeline related to racism. Note approximate dates when events or people have influenced
what you think about prejudice and race, negatively
or positively. Share with each other the very first event
or person on your timeline. How were you shaped by
the incident?

8. Sing together "Lift every voice and sing."

3

Misreading the Text
Genesis 9:18-27

*A furious Noah cuts off his son Ham's descendants
from the family inheritance and declares that they will
forever serve Ham's brother Shem and his family. For
centuries, this story about Hamitic people (Africans)
was used to support the institution of slavery. It has
been one of history's most unfortunate misuses of
the Bible, which is, in the end, the story of God's saving and liberating acts in the world, not an apology
for slavery.*

Personal Preparation

1. Reflect upon the biblical teaching you have received. Did
   anyone ever give you a biblical rationale for believing
   that one race is better than others? What scriptures
   were used to teach racism? What scriptures were used
   to teach equality?

2. Before reading Genesis 9, sometimes called the "Curse
   of Ham," review the sequence of events in your mind or
   on paper as you remember them. Who were the major
   characters? What is the plot? What do you think the
   text means?

3. Then read Genesis 9 (especially verses 20-28). What did
   you remember correctly? What parts of the story did you
   miss? Draw a family tree of Noah's family, including
   Ham, Shem, and Japheth. Also include Ham's sons: Cush,

Mizraim, Phut, and Canaan. Look at a Bible map to see what lands each inherited.

4. Read Psalm 13 lamenting the anguish of the oppressed. The psalmist laments, but also trusts. Try to identify both actions (lament and trust) in the psalm. Read the psalm as a victim of racism would read it.

5. Sing or read the African American spiritual "Calvary" (p. 105) in your prayer and meditation this week.

Understanding

In his book *Slaves in the Family*, Edward Ball takes a journey to his past, interviewing his relatives whose ancestors owned slaves and the descendants of the slaves who lived on the Ball family's extensive network of plantations in South Carolina. On his journey, Ball found a poem penned by a Ball family cousin, Cousin Kate, sometime before emancipation. In it she makes reference to Genesis 9, the most famous passage used to support slavery, the story of Noah and his sons. A portion of the poem goes like this:

> Returning, one perchance may careless roam
> To where the Negroes have their village home;
> Its cleanly rows, of cottages so neat;
> The hearty welcomes that your presence greet;
> The quiet calmness that pervades the spot,
> Show that the sons of Canaan dark, are not
> The poor depressed mortals they are thought,
> Tho' they say "master," and are sold and bought!

Misuse of the Bible

At the same time, great abolitionist preachers like Sojourner Truth were railing against the institution of slavery and preaching that God led the slaves out of bondage in Egypt, southern white ministers were justifying slavery using the story of Noah's sons and their own biblical interpretation of other texts. They contended that God had "ordained" a hierarchical system of human beings in which white men were closest to God and people of color were lower than wives and children of white men, somehow forgetting that all peoples of the Bible were people of color.

To some extent, proponents of slavery and discrimination can find basis for their views. After all, the biblical witness is ambivalent about slavery. The Hebrew Bible and the New Testament take slavery for granted as part of the social order of the times. It's true that the societies of the biblical world not only included the institutions of slavery and mandatory servanthood, but also structured culture in a strict hierarchical world order. In spite of Jesus' powerful talk of freedom in Christ, Paul's writings assume that slavery was a given in the societies of the world.

Even though slavery as an institution does not exist in North America, in some subtle and not so subtle ways the hierarchical social structure of the biblical world is still accepted as the social norm. Biblical texts are still used and misused to support a structure that devalues people of color here and around the world. The task before us requires a reading of the text that hears the gospel without the "noise" of society and culture that surrounds it. That's not easy!

The story of Noah and his sons stands out as the principal biblical text justifying the institution of slavery and overtly racist attitudes of some Christians. Even today many white supremacist groups use this text as the foundation of their belief in the superiority of the white race. Most often they use Genesis 9 as proof that people whose skin is dark are descendants of Ham and doomed to slavery.

Uncovering the Text

This text (Gen. 9:20-28) illuminates what happens when we read biblical texts, especially texts from the Old Testament, by laying our social and cultural circumstances and biases on it. Instead of imposing something on the Bible story that isn't there, it is important that we examine it carefully for what it says in its own context.

Principally, the story of Noah tells of the reshaping of the inheritance of the sons of Noah after the flood. According to the text, Noah had three sons: Shem, Ham and Japheth. Ham was the father of Canaan, ancestor of the Canaanites. In this episode Noah is drunk and lies asleep naked. Ham sees the condition of his father and tells his brothers. There being a prohibition against seeing someone naked in the Old Testament or, as some scholars think in this case, of having sexual relations with a parent (euphemistically called "uncovering"), the brothers, Shem and Japheth, take a garment and walk backward into Noah's tent, so as not to see Noah, and cover their father's nakedness.

When Noah wakes up from his drunken sleep, he realizes Ham's transgression and says, "Cursed be Canaan [Ham's son]; lowest of slaves shall he be to his brother" (Gen. 9:25). The blessings of Noah are to be received by Shem, whose eventual ancestor is Abraham, the heir of the promised land and people and covenant. Japheth is to be given a place within Shem's family, but Canaan, the son of Ham, loses his part of the inheritance because of the sin of his father. Moreover, he is to be the slave of these brothers.

This passage is often mistakenly called "the Curse of Ham." Those who lay the curse on Ham therefore extend the curse to all Ham's descendants, that is to all black people of African/Hamitic descent. A closer reading of the text, however, reveals that in fact only Canaan, one of Ham's four sons, was cursed (Gen. 9:25). The other sons: Cush, Mizraim, and Phut were not cursed. Genesis 10 tells us that the descendants of Ham's other sons peopled the land of North and Northeast Africa. The descendants of Ham were Cush (biblical Ethiopia, or modern day Sudan), Mizraim (Egypt), Phut (Libya) and Canaan (Palestine/Israel).

The result of the blessings and curses in this text were that the people of Canaan (Israel/Palestine) were to be servants, while the descendants of Shem, including Abraham, were to inherit the land as part of the blessing of Noah. In its own context, this text justifies the conquest of Palestine by the Israelites and in fact has nothing to do with using "Negroes" or black people as slaves.

Where did we go wrong in reading Genesis 9? It's not that the story isn't useful as a story. We have told many other Bible stories, including the exodus from Egypt, to illustrate a point of faith. That's not the issue here. The issue is the failure to read this text in light of other witnesses of the Bible. The exodus story clearly contributes to the Bible's complete story of salvation. In its larger context, Noah and his family illustrate how sin distorts the order of things as they were intended to be. As Genesis scholar Gene Roop notes, "Enslavement distorts the vision of God's creation as much as male/female relationships lived in domination and subordination (3:16) and the murder of one brother by another (4:8)." Only apart from this larger context could anyone conclude that Genesis 9 is a defense of slavery.

The Idolatry of Racism

Racism is idolatrous. As human beings we have a tendency to think we are God and to lift ourselves above others by putting others down. We are entirely capable of constructing a theological hierarchy in which the most powerful people (usually folk like us) are closer to God, while others not like us are more distant. It is a mentality that always makes the powerful majority feel good about themselves at the expense of others. In this way we justify our own access to privileges and resources that are denied to others. But the use of any biblical text to do this is idolatry and a misreading of the text.

It is important to remember that the sins of racism, discrimination, and idolatry are ever present realities in the North American context and not just a problem of the past. In order for racism to live on, it becomes a whole way of thinking that affects how we do business, what we learn, and how we read the Bible. So the misreading of Genesis 9 is as predictable as it is regrettable.

The Church and Slavery

Long before the beginnings of African American slave experience, the church debated the institution of slavery, the bottom rung in the hierarchical social system. An early theology of slavery can be found in the writings of Augustine, the early fifth-century bishop of Hippo. Augustine basically uses the arguments common in his day. He believes that all people were equal before the fall; however, the result of the sinfulness of humankind is the establishment of "institutions of coercion," including slavery. After the fall and with the beginning of free will, people will not voluntarily be good. Augustine reasons that people need structures to help them do what is right. Therefore, Augustine believes that slaves should accept their station in life as a good thing and be obedient and kind toward their masters.

Like Paul, Augustine believes that the worst slavery is the enslavement to sin, and it is this belief that shaped the church's theology for centuries to follow. Perhaps more importantly for us today, Augustine continued to accept the highly structured social system, both within and outside the church as a given of created order. Any time society is structured in that way, someone is placed higher and others are placed lower.

Although few people in America believe in the institution of slavery, there are those who persist in believing that white people have genetic superiority and that people of color are naturally inferior. The accepted hierarchy of social structure places people of color at the lowest end of our society, including in the church.

A Religious Legacy

Racism shaped the American mind, and the institution of slavery was the social and economic expression of that racism for more than three hundred years. The institution of slavery is gone but the mind-set still affects people of color today. Like Mennonites and Amish who tell the ageless stories of persecution and martyrdom and Jews who recount the horrors of the holocaust, African Americans still feel the effects of slavery and the discrimination of the past and present.

To understand how deeply the effects of racial idolatry and biblical misuse run, we have only to listen to stories of African American families who know the accounts of their ancestors who lived and died within the institutions of slavery. We can see the legacy even in African American family reunions which often bring together one family with several surnames, the result of families being separated and sold as chattel. Taking on the last name of a new owner, one family member may have a different name than any other member of the immediate family.

Hatred between races is still common. In suburban Greenwich, Connecticut, five white high school seniors encoded "kill all niggers" into the school's yearbook captions. Their only defense was that they didn't really mean it. In another instance, three black teens killed a white teenager who rode in a truck displaying the Confederate flag. Their defense was that peer pressure made them kill.

What should be the response of Christians? During the civil rights movement, white and black Christians joined hands to bring an end to the laws and social norms that overtly discriminated against African Americans. But today the church remains mostly silent. Few churches are successful at creating an atmosphere where people of diverse races and cultures feel comfortable worshiping together.

One response Christians can make is to correct misreadings of the text when they have a chance. Be quick to point out that Genesis 9 does not justify slavery or a belief in the inferiority of people of color. Quite the contrary, the central theme of the Old Testament is the exodus. This important saving act of God shows us people who themselves suffered the institution of slavery and were liberated by God, despite their sinfulness, to become the chosen people. The Hebrew people were lead out of slavery by a liberating, loving God.

And what about slavery passages in the New Testament in Paul's writings? They also must be seen against other witnesses to the gospel. Jesus commanded us to love our neighbors. There are no limits to race placed on that commandment. We live in a world filled with hierarchical systems that give people of color a lower social status. Let our congregations not reflect that system. Rather, let us reflect the message that Jesus calls us to overcome the barriers of race that divide people. Our faith can make us bold enough to declare that God loves all people and empowers us to be messengers of that love. Like many Christians throughout the centuries, we must be activists, people actively promoting racial understanding and opposing institutions of racism.

Discussion and Action

1. In the past, the Bible was used to justify slavery. How do we justify racism today?

2. What is your earliest memory from your religious education about races? How has your understanding changed since then, if at all? What caused you to change?

3. Describe an experience that you had with an individual of another race. What surprised you about the experience? What did you learn?

4. Make a list of topics or issues featured in the news today, including racism. What biblical texts have people used for or against these issues? In which cases do you think the Bible has been misinterpreted? How widespread is the problem of misinterpreting the Bible?

5. Make a list of people who you think model being good neighbors to people of other races. Your list could include famous people, like Mother Teresa and Barbara Jordan. It could also include people from your own community who reach out to others. If it is a local person(s), take time to send a thank you note from the group.

6. Break into pairs or groups of three. Take turns saying in one sentence what the Bible is all about. Go around again and say in one sentence what the Bible says generally to you about racism.

7. If available, review your denomination's materials on racism and discrimination. Where should the church go from here?

8. Sing or read the spiritual "Calvary" (p. 105) together as a prayer.

4

The Subtlety of Racism
Matthew 7:1-5

Racism is not limited to hooded Knights of the Ku Klux Klan or members of the Christian Identity movement. Of course, burning crosses and hate mail are overt signs of racism in our society, but a lot of racism comes in a more subtle fashion that is difficult to quantify and challenge.

Personal Preparation

1. Read Matthew 7:1-5. Jesus taught the disciples about judging. Does this text mean that we should not confront evil when we see it? How does this passage apply when we see evil or an injustice being done? What logs do you have in your own eyes? What could you do to pluck them out?

2. What do you think is the most obvious form of racism in America today? What is the least obvious, most subtle form? Which happens more frequently? Which is worse in your estimation? Why?

3. What do you do when someone makes a racial or ethnic joke in your presence? How do the jokes make you feel? How would the people who are the butt of the joke feel about the jokes?

4. Sing or pray the words to "This little light of mine." Often considered a children's song, this spiritual reflects the determination of one person to make the world a little

better. The light of God shines through each action we take. Pray that your light will shine in your work, in your family, and in your church.

Understanding

The flashing lights on the police car lit up the entire area as we pulled over. All five of us teenagers were concerned about what would happen next. When the officer came to the window, he ordered me, only me, out of the vehicle. I wasn't even driving. I was sitting between two friends in the back seat. There I was with my hands on the car and my legs spread. My friend who was driving got a speeding ticket, but I was the one embarrassed. I was the only one pulled out. I was also the only one in the car who was black.

I am proud that my name is Roberto. I am named after my grandfather, a caring and hardworking man. I love to hear my mother and others call my name because it reminds me of who I am and who my family is. But school is different. On the first day of school, the teacher called me "Bobby." I told her that my name was "Roberto," but she said that "Bobby" is much easier. It is not easier for me. I'm not the only one — "Esteban" became "Steve"; "Maria" became "Mary." My teacher does not understand. My name is Roberto and I'm proud of my name.

Even before looking at my grades and my SAT scores, the counselor suggested that I consider the general high school graduation plan, not the pre-college graduation plan. I said I wanted to go to college. The counselor looked surprised. "You might want to consider vocational school," he said. I felt like he was saying that I should not even think about college. Are all black people too stupid for college?

All alone, I stepped into the elevator and pushed the button for the fifth floor. When the elevator door opened on the second floor, four young black men entered. As the doors closed, I panicked. I told myself not to be afraid, but my heart started to beat fast. Quickly I pushed the button to exit at the third floor. I was so relieved to get out of there. Just think what could have happened!

———

I can remember it like it was yesterday. I was in the fourth grade, just browsing in the store. That is when I noticed that several people were following me — and me alone — through the store, making sure I wouldn't take anything.

Acts of prejudice and discrimination like these are subtle. They're not extreme. They're not overt. Many people who commit them are not even conscious they are discriminating, like the teacher who insists on anglicizing non-English names. They're ingrained habits or reactions based on stereotypes, like the white woman who flinched at the thought of being in an elevator with black men.

The times that Americans are most aware of the destructive power of these "little" racisms, however, is when tables are turned and someone in the majority is slighted. Troy Duster, a sociologist at the University of California at Berkeley, tells of a woman named Cheryl Hopwood, "a white female who sued the University of Texas Law School, claiming she had been the victim of racial discrimination because she was not admitted even though she had higher test scores than students of color who were admitted. The appellate court directed the lower court to consider damages to Hopwood, and she is seeking more than $1 million from the state. In all these decades of racial exclusion, no court in this nation has ever been directed to consider damages for a single student of color" (*Mother Jones*, September/October 1997). Justice for one reveals a sad, pervasive injustice for others.

More Than a Perception

Not surprisingly, victims of race discrimination will see more quickly the injustice of subtle racism than will the majority, and unfortunately, they'll more quickly be accused of exaggerating the truth. But a recent poll in the United States confirms that there is a significant difference between the way African Americans and people of European descent see racism. While a majority of white people thought that racism was not a significant factor in the lives of Americans, a majority of blacks believed that they live with significant racism. What accounts for this discrepancy in perception?

Racial groups see racism in different degrees depending on how each experiences or doesn't experience discrimination. People of color feel the daily sting of small incidents, piercing reminders of racism, while most white Americans rarely experience discrimination and find it hard to believe that it is as pervasive as it is. Our friends, Barbara and Larson, can testify to the deep wounds caused by small, daily incidences of racism, incidences that seem downright implausible to many whites. Barbara frequently works away from her desk, out in the community. When her husband Larson, an African American, decided to surprise her for lunch one rare day when he thought she was in the office, he quickly looked over the cars in the parking lot for Barbara's car, a good clue that she was in, before going up several flights of stairs to Barbara's office. Just as he arrived, dressed neatly for his job, three young white men, dressed very poorly and looking scruffy, came through the front door and asked Larson for directions to another office in the same building. They assumed a black man must be the doorman.

Then shortly after Larson arrived at Barbara's office, a city police officer approached Larson and Barbara. An anonymous fellow office worker had phoned city police about a suspicious young black man who was "cruising the parking lot and peering through car windows." No one had noticed the far more suspicious looking young white men. No one had asked Larson what he was doing in the parking lot. Assumptions about his presence were made that were humiliating and embarrassing. But the greater pain comes from the stereotyping that Larson battles every day. Because of subtle racism, he is never as free as a white man to move about or be himself.

All of us discriminate in subtle ways, especially when we make automatic judgments based on biases handed to us by family, society, media, and even the church. The white woman who fears getting on an elevator with black men does not react out of experience but out of a droning social message that black men are dangerous. The clerk in the store watches the Asian boys in the store not because she knows them to be thieves, but because she has seen in movies and heard among neighbors that Asians are sneaky. The officer who singles out the black youth in a car of white youth has no real reason to suspect him above the others, but does so out of biases learned in the surrounding culture.

Judging Ourselves

While these subtle forms of racism are perpetuated often out of habit, they are, nonetheless, judgments. Even if we simply give our lazy acceptance to the way things are, we've made a judgment. We've decided that the way things are is the way they should be. In the Sermon on the Mount, Jesus cautions against certain kinds of judging (Matt. 7:1-5). He does not prohibit us from judging at all, but from judging too harshly or judging with an excessive "measure." Matthew is quick to point out that Jesus commands us to judge idolaters and those who offend other Christians (Matt. 18), but he points out here that it is the "measure" of the judgment that is important. When judgment is used to elevate ourselves, put someone else down, or avenge some slight instead of gauging whether Jesus is at the center of our lives, it is a sin.

Jesus is not just preaching good sense when he says that we will be judged in the same measure that we judge. It might be true that those we judge could point fingers of judgment right back at us, but the greater judgment we will receive is God's judgment. Those who have been judgmental and uncompassionate prove that they have little commitment to being followers of Christ and will be judged accordingly. As God has been merciful to us, even when we deserved judgment, we ought to be merciful to others.

Of course, each of us is prejudiced. It is impossible to grow up in this society without some bias, some fear, some concern about people who are different. However, as Christians, literally Christ followers, we are challenged to use love to overcome the fears and hate we have learned. It's not enough to simply denounce overt racism. It's not enough to lay blame on history or prevailing social biases. Each of us needs to confess our own sin, to pluck out that log in our own eye, and work to overcome our prejudices. With the pervasiveness of subtle racism and the difficulty of contradicting old biases, this is not an easy task. That's apparently why Jesus calls the sins of others mere "specks" and our own sins "logs"!

Some Christians attempt to avoid judgment altogether, but the judgment Jesus is talking about here is God's judgment, the kind none of us will escape. We're all sinners. If we think we can escape, we are the hypocrites that Jesus names. We see sin in others but not in ourselves. We think that others are prejudiced and racist, but we are not. Self-examination will quickly reveal whether we are faithful and whether we have put Jesus at the center of our lives.

Plucking Out Logs

Our reluctance to deal with our own logs came home to me in the experience of a friend who works with a denominational staff in the area of racism awareness. To raise the board members' awareness of their own racism, she noted how few people of color sat in higher levels of employment within the organization. When she pointed out that few minorities even held seats on the board, one particular board member was offended by what felt like an accusation. Several other white men and women said, "We have no significant power." To emphasize the subtle prejudice implied in their attitudes, our friend followed up by counting the minutes that each board member talked at a board meeting. Not only was there a small percentage of minority members on the board, but those minority board members spoke an even smaller percentage of the time. No wonder some of these board members felt that they were simply "token" members elected to cover up the real power of the white people on the board.

White members of the denominational board hypothesized about the reasons that the organization lacked minority participation. One person said, "Minority people don't have the 'patience' for our long, detailed board meetings." Another person felt that meetings are not part of "their culture." The more likely reasons are that views, unless they are in line with the prevailing views of the board, are not heard and respected, which, ironically, is the reason for diversifying an organization. Moreover, minority members are not always truly welcome to participate fully. Boards are sometimes guilty of attracting a variety of faces to their organizations more for appearance than for a true interest in diverse opinion. In that case physical differences are valued, but philosophical differences are not. Then there is always the issue of access. Who is eligible to serve? Is some minority participation limited because of the economic requirements for the position, for example, the requirement of taking workdays off midweek or paying for transportation?

The subtlety of racism makes discrimination in general very difficult to overcome. Martin Luther King, Jr. often spoke about how much more difficult it is to confront subtle racism than overt racism. The artist, Judy Chicago, in her study of the Holocaust reflects that part of the horror in Nazi Germany was the banality, the ordinariness, and the subtlety of hate and evil. She noted that across the street from the gas chambers were ordinary homes and families. For those outside the concentration camps, life was all too plain and ordinary. Those who participated in the evils of that system had families and homes not unlike their neighbors and friends.

The subtlety of racism should not be dismissed because it is hard to see at times. In fact, it should be examined seriously because of the ability of small hatreds and biases to erode society. But more than the social consequences of racism, Christians ought to be worried about racism's consequences to faith. When we think we have avoided God's judgment by being kind and just, but have not challenged the subtle, institutionalized forms of racism in which we all participate (even unwittingly), we are guilty of at least two sins. We are arrogant for thinking we are above judgment and we are hypocrites for thinking we have not sinned when we have. The Christian community is stronger if it quickly searches for the log and plucks it out. Only then can we all claim the moral upper hand and enjoy the benefits of God's diverse world.

Often minority people are accused of being overly sensitive to racial issues. But when minority people point out examples of institutional racism, white people are generally offended and have hurt feelings. But is not honesty the loving and truthful way to curb racism in our lives and in our institutions? Should we not put our personal feelings aside and examine our behavior and attitudes as we try to make our families and institutions more reflective of the interracial family of God? Only as we overcome all the subtle ways that racism invades our culture and society can we enjoy the benefits of the wonderful diverse nature of God's children.

Discussion and Action

1. Take turns telling about the first time you were aware of your racial background? At what age did most of you become aware? How often do you think of your skin color? Do you think some racial groups are more aware of their color than other groups? Why or why not?

2. Write a sentence to contribute to a group prayer confessing your own prejudices and ways that you participate in racism. Open your heart to tell God about those feelings that are judgmental, stereotypical, and unfair. When everyone is finished writing, enter a time of prayer. Take turns reading your sentences. Pause between each for reflection.

3. Racism can be overt or subtle. A 1996 study of mortgage lenders showed that lenders still reject black applicants twice as often as whites, despite tougher enforcement of fair lending rules. According to data released by the federal government, banks, savings institutions, credit unions, and mortgage companies turned down 48.8 percent of applications for home purchase loans received from blacks and 24.1 percent from whites. The denial rates were 34.4 percent for Hispanics of all races, 13.8 percent for Asians, and 50.2 percent for Native Americans. Lenders don't believe this is racism, because rejections are based on

individual credit histories and indebtedness. Overall, is this racism? Would you call this overt or subtle racism?

4. Tell about a personal experience with subtle racism, such as a racial joke, an injustice, a comment, or a business decision. What was your reaction to the event? How did others react? If the incident went unnoticed by others, why?

5. Watch a video such as *Eyes on the Prize: America's Civil Rights Years 1954–1965* or *Viva la Causa! 500 Years of Chicano History* or *True Colors*. Afterward discuss what you learned. What stereotypes do the documentaries help you give up? How does history change the way you see the problem of racism today?

6. Read aloud the short vignettes at the beginning of the Understanding section. What does each voice say about racism and prejudice? How does subtle racism affect each person? What can be done to change the situation?

7. Talk about Barbara and Larson. How should they have reacted to the incident in Barbara's office? How can they prevent a similar thing from happening in the future? Should Larson change his behavior simply because it is easily misunderstood by white people? Should Barbara confront her colleagues?

8. From your preparation, tell what you think is the most obvious form of racism in America today. What is the least obvious, most subtle form? Which happens more frequently? Which is worse, in your estimation? Why?

9. What new awareness do you have of prejudices and discrimination in your community after thinking about subtle racism? What can be done locally to overcome those subtle racisms?

5

Racism and Hate Crimes
1 John 2:7-11

Incidents of overt racism have been on the increase since the 1970s, when a general disapproval of race discrimination in society forced racism into more subtle forms. A resurgence of the Ku Klux Klan and other hate groups, including those who claim to be Christian, indicates new levels of race hatred in America. How can people of faith respond to irrational hate?

Personal Preparation

1. Read 1 John 2:7-11. When is it hardest for you to love? Who would you include among your "brothers and sisters"? Is there anyone you are not required to love? Who?

2. Review recent newspapers. Clip articles that describe overt racism. What surprises you about the stories you find? Check your local library for "Intelligence Project" published by the Southern Poverty Law Center. The "Intelligence Project" is a regular newsletter for law enforcement and human rights groups.

3. In what ways has overt racism touched your community? What was your response?

4. Prepare yourself for this difficult topic by reviewing the words or singing "When the storms of life are raging." This hymn reminds us that we need to be strong in the face of adversity and that God stands with us. Pray that

God will give us patience and courage to speak out and face difficult situations.

Understanding

John King was a prisoner in a Texas penitentiary for a probation violation on a robbery conviction. Already a Klan fan, King learned more about white supremacists groups and philosophy in prison where he corresponded secretly with other prisoners. He and several others had a goal of organizing a chapter of a Klan-related group called the Confederate Knights of America when he got out of prison. Initiation into the group was to be the murder of a person of color. While King was free on parole in 1998, he and two others stopped an unsuspecting black man named James Byrd who was walking down the road in the early morning. They took him to a secluded piece of woods where there was a short struggle. Then the three men chained Byrd by the ankles to the back of their pickup truck and dragged the innocent man for several miles until his body was dismembered, worn to the bones, and he was dead.

Authorities immediately linked King to evidence at the murder site and to a note that was intercepted during his prison term that talked about the murder plans. At the trial where he was found guilty in short order, the dead man's sister made an eloquent public statement, saying she would not hate John King, for in doing so she would be no better than he.

Out of the Past

Until recently we thought of race atrocities as a thing of the past. At the turn of the twentieth century, poverty, competition for jobs, waves of immigration, and suspicion of Jews and foreigners fueled racial conflict that ended in horrible rioting, clashes with police, mob violence, murder, vigilantism, and lynchings. A famous murder case in 1913 in Atlanta, Georgia, was typical of the era. Mary Phagan, a young white girl, was found murdered in the pencil factory where she worked. While all evidence pointed to a black man who also worked at the factory, the prosecutor decided that Leo Frank, the Jewish factory superintendent, would pay for the crime, for, as a minister in town said, "This one old Negro would be poor atonement for the life of this innocent girl." Despite all the evidence otherwise, the prosecutor succeeded in concocting a case and whipping up public support for a conviction. Leo Frank was railroaded to a guilty verdict and sentenced to hang. The governor commuted the death sentence, but an angry mob stormed the prison, took Frank out and demanded a confession. Frank's story convinced most of the mob that he was not guilty, but having set out to kill him, they could not leave without doing the job, so they lynched him in a tree and left his body for all to see true "justice."

We'd like to believe that such things could not happen today, but, sad to say, hate crimes and overt racism are not the problem of some other generation. Overtly racial incidents like black church burnings, James Byrd's murder, the police beatings of Rodney King and Reginald Denney, race riots in Los Angeles between Koreans and African Americans, and the violence between Brooklyn blacks and Hasidic Jews are just a few of the incidents that remind us racism is alive and growing in America. The litany of overtly racist hate crimes shows that these are more than anecdotal episodes. And for every incident we know of from the news and police blotters, there are many that go unreported. As each one of us is touched by an experience, we're beginning to realize that overt racism is common.

Abundant Hatred

Hatred is a powerful motivator that turns ordinary people into monsters. The prosecutor in the Leo Frank case, for instance, played on a community's underlying dislike and suspicion of Jews to create an unstoppable force of irrational hatred. Or, more recently, take the example of the Freeman family in Allentown, Pennsylvania. Things went terribly wrong in the family when their two sons Bryan and David fell under the influence of Skinhead hatemongers. Bryan and David Freeman still lived with their parents near Allentown when they started attending nearby rallies that drew as many as 300 Neo-Nazi Skinheads, Aryan Nations members, and militant

Klansmen. The boys shaved their heads, acquired Nazi tattoos, and began using alcohol and drugs.

Their parents were concerned and sought help for the boys. However, the boys responded by calling their mother a "race traitor." David actually told her he was "going to enjoy killing her." In February 1995, the boys carried out their threats. With their cousin Nelson looking on, the boys beat and stabbed their parents and their 11-year-old brother to death. The boys pleaded guilty and have been sentenced to life in prison. We reel to think how children could be convinced not only to hate people different from them, but to hate even their own family—for not hating. Unfortunately, their actions are not unique, and their belief in white supremacy is infecting more and more American young people.

Many Christians would guess that overt racism has lessened in recent years. In reality there has been a dramatic increase. The "Intelligence Project" keeps close track of cross-burnings in the United States. A few of the incidents from 1998 alone are listed below. Note that they occurred many places outside the deep south.

Long Island, New York
A young man was charged with falsely reporting a bias incident and setting a cross on fire after he allegedly burned a cross in front of his parents' home.

Center Point, Alabama
A cross was burned at a white woman's mobile home.

Phoenix, Arizona
A 19-year-old boy was sentenced to 30 months in prison for his part in a cross-burning at a black family's residence in May 1997.

Cheraw, South Carolina.
Three young men and a juvenile allegedly burned a cross at a man's residence and broke into his home and vandalized it.

Lancaster, California
A cross was burned at a black woman's residence.

Lodi, California
A cross was burned at a high school.

Augusta, Georgia
A cross draped in a Klan robe was erected at a high school.

Coeur d'Alene, Idaho
A cross was burned outside the residence of three white college students. A doll with the letters "KKK" written on it was also left on the front porch.

Bloomington, Illinois
A cross was burned on property rented by a black resident.

Cross-burnings are an ironic symbol of Christian fidelity. They demonstrate that the Ku Klux Klan sees itself as a Christian organization with a mandate for biblical fidelity. Klan propaganda quotes biblical texts on racial purity, though, oddly, no one in the Bible is caucasian. As Bible scholar Cain Hope Felder notes, "Moses was born in Africa, he lived in Africa, and in fact, he never made it as far as Palestine." People of the Bible came from North Africa, the Middle East, Asia, and Mediterranean cultures. They ranged in color from black to bronze and brown. Jesus, himself, was a Middle Easterner. Burning crosses in the name of purity is obviously a complete perversion of Christianity's most sacred symbol. The Klan has taken the cross and turned it into a symbol of intimidation, hatred, and fear. What sort of Christianity is it, we have to ask, in which people can be faithful and utterly hateful at the same time?

In recent years, cross-burnings have turned into whole church burnings. Between January 1995 and July 1996 alone, 85 churches were burned by arsonists in America. At least 58 of those were predominately black churches. Journalist Anthony Walton points out that only ten percent of the population of the U.S. is African American, yet more than half of the church arsons are in black churches. The statistics point to something more than coincidence. Even if the fires are not a conspiracy of the Klan or other white supremacy group, but are an unrelated string of events carried out by rednecks, drunks, and thieves, it is telltale that African Americans consistently are their victims.

Overt racism does not end with burning crosses and churches. It includes assaults, bombings, harassment, intimidation, and vandalism. The national information network on racism helps us see trends in the occurrence of hate crimes and overt racism and to awaken Christians to the crisis.

Here is a sampling of the sort of incidents that watchdog organizations tracked in 1998. They cover a wide range in the degree of violence and destructiveness, but all are clear, outright cases of racism. They signal the breadth and depth of attitudes about race in the society at large.

Mobile, Alabama
An 18-year-old white male was sentenced to five years in federal prison after pleading guilty to arson and racially motivated vandalism at a black church in June 1997.

Denver, Colorado
A young woman was convicted of first-degree murder after her Skinhead acquaintance killed a police officer in November.

Clover, South Carolina
Copies of a racist, threatening letter containing a Klan slogan were sent to six black high school students.

San Diego, California
A 19-year-old pleaded guilty to the August stabbing of an American Indian-Hispanic man whom he believed was black.

Athens, Georgia
A sign with the letters "KKK" on it was hung on the mailbox at a black family's residence.

Coeur d'Alene, Idaho
A Former Aryan Nations security chief was charged with aggravated assault and using a weapon to commit a crime. He allegedly drove a pickup used by Aryan Nations members to chase and shoot at a woman's car in July, forcing the car to crash into a ditch.

East St. Louis, Illinois
A white supremacist was convicted of conspiracy for conspiring to bomb several human rights organizations and public buildings, assassinate a civil rights lawyer, kill a federal judge, rob banks and poison water supplies, and possess unregistered weapons.

Bronx, New York
A 15-year-old girl was sentenced to six years in prison after she

pleaded guilty to first-degree assault for her part in slashing a Jewish man in the face with a knife and using anti-Semitic epi-
thets in August.

Even as this book was being prepared, two troubled white students at the homogeneous Columbine High School in Littleton,
Colorado, schemed for more than a year to assault their classmates, including blacks. In all, they killed twelve students and
one teacher before they died themselves. After the rampage, authorities found a number of homemade explosive devices planted
inside and outside the school.

Claiming Christianity

The list of overt racist incidents could go on for pages. It should
take only a few mentions, however, for Christians to become concerned about race hatred, violence, and intimidation. But we
should be even more concerned by the rise of Christian identity
groups who claim the same faith as we do, but who are outwardly,
proudly, stridently racist. These groups, often calling themselves
"church," offer historical and biblical justifications for white supremacy, race hatred, and violence. Adhering to "God's law,"
members of these groups often use criminal activity such as robbery and arson to threaten opponents and finance their groups.
Often these groups are quite powerful and are able to intimidate
those who disagree with them.

How is it that the Christian message can be so perverted? How
can the biblical text be so misinterpreted that it is used to justify
violence, murder, and hatred? What kind of hatred can twist the
central biblical mandate to love each other into a commandment
to torment or kill? How should we as Christians behave toward
the hateful and the racists who share our claim to Christianity?

Having faced hatred within the church community, the author
of 1, 2, and 3 John addresses these questions for Christians. Not
so long after the death of Jesus and the first appearance of the
Gospels, factions arose in the church, each claiming a corner on
the truth about Jesus. One controversy that arose was disagreement over Jesus' nature, some saying he was wholly divine, others saying he was wholly human. The Gospel of John more than

the other Gospels emphasizes the divinity of Jesus. The first chapter of the Gospel tells how Jesus was descended to the world from God, and before his earthly life he was with God in the divine, even from the beginning of time. "In the beginning was the Word, and the Word was with God, and the Word was God" (John 1:1).

Likely written by the same John, the first letter of John is in some ways a corrective or a response to those who read the Gospel and began to believe that Jesus was only Spirit, only Divine. While it was true that Jesus was the Son of God, John wanted also to say that Jesus was human and his teachings are not mere instructions on how to transcend earthly life; they tell us how to live in this world as a follower of Jesus.

One of the most central teachings of the New Testament is to love one another. This is the commandment to which John refers in 1 John 2:7-11. "Beloved, I am writing you no new commandment, but an old commandment that you have had from the beginning" (2:7). John brings up the familiar teaching because, evidently, there were factions antagonistic to the teaching in John's community. They claimed to be Christians ("in the light"), but they were hateful ("in the dark").

In Matthew, Mark, and Luke, Jesus commands that we not only love one another within the Christian community, but we should also love our enemies. John, however, seems to counsel only that we love "one another," those within our own fold. It depends somewhat on how we interpret the terms "brother and sister." Are brothers and sisters the believers in our congregations or are they others, even the ones "in the dark"? John apparently felt his detractors were beyond the pale and were lost in darkness. To John, their claims of faith were illegitimate. They could not hate and be part of the faith. With his remaining faithful students, John counseled love among themselves and distance and disdain for the unfaithful. But taken together with the other Gospel writers, the biblical witness seems to teach that we must love everyone, even enemies, even believers "in the dark." In other words, we are commanded to love the hateful and not be hateful ourselves.

How do hate groups construe the text to love one another otherwise? They do not deny the commandment to love, but they define "one another" as their members. Only insiders need be included. For example, "loving one another" means loving only white people, or one racial group. Faith is not the criterion for membership in their fellowship. Being of the "chosen" race is the distinguishing characteristic of a member. To them, people of other races are not Christians and white supremacist are not required to treat them as such.

To us, the logic is inconceivable. To hate groups, it is highly rational. But as the eighteenth-century writer Samuel Johnson reminds us, "Prejudice not being founded on reason cannot be removed by argument." Where reason will not help us, love may. As for James Byrd's sister, love may be the thing that keeps us from sinking to the level of barbarism of our hateful brothers and sisters.

In the face of rising membership in hate groups, it is important that Christians, especially white Christians, witness to brothers and sisters who are overt racists, proclaiming that God does not discriminate by race. What's more, the church should expose the error of those who pervert the Christian message of love, making it a message of race hatred and white superiority. We all use scripture to our own ends at times. But the one unmistakable charge of the gospel is that we must love God and others. All the rest hangs on this. For the sake of the kingdom and real people's lives, Christians cannot afford to be silent. It is through the voice of the church and Christians around the world that the message of love and caring for all will be told.

Discussion and Action

1. Why do people hate? Talk also about why it is sometimes hard to love. Are any of the reasons you have shared based on race? Why or why not?

2. Samuel Johnson says, "Prejudice not being founded on reason cannot be removed by argument." Talk about this statement. To what extent are acts of overt racism backed by reason? What reasons do racists give? What arguments

counter their claims? If argument is useless, what other ways can Christians counter the logic of racists?

3. List examples of overt racism and hate crimes that have occurred during the last few years in your community or in the nation. How did the community respond? If you wish to say, how did you respond? Does it seem as if acts of overt racism polarize your community or bring different people closer together? Why?

4. Discuss hate crimes and the role of the media. How well or how poorly does the media report overt racial incidents? To what extent does the media reflect back to us what is going on in race relations in the country? To what extent does it propel racism by the way it reports? And to what extent does the media underreport racial incidents?

5. Make it a priority to get to know people of other races personally. Talk about ways to make friends across race lines, such as sharing worship, working on community committees together, starting a racism watchdog service for your community, inviting people to your home for a meal, and ensuring your children have playmates from other races. Make a personal connection that crosses society's usual boundaries. If you have already done this, talk about your experiences. Help others in the group get started.

6. What do you think should be the attitude of Christians toward overt racists? When should we keep them at arm's length and not associate with them? When should we associate with them more to foster change?

7. Pray as a group for an end to hate crimes. Pray that each person will see the love of God in the actions of others, regardless of racial origin. Pray that we can recognize each other as children of God.

8. Close by singing "When the storms of life are raging."

6

The Costs and Profits of Racism
1 Corinthians 12:12-26

*Racism costs our society both figuratively and liter-
ally. Segregation in the South raised the cost of public
buildings by demanding separate facilities, such as
restrooms and drinking fountains, for non-whites.
Today we still suffer from the loss of talents and
gifts of minority members. Long ago in the Bible
Paul told us that the whole body suffers without the
gifts of diverse members.*

Personal Preparation

1. Read 1 Corinthians 12:12-26. How does it apply to your
   congregation? How diverse is your congregation? How
   similar are you in ethnic and racial background? In what
   ways does each member depend on the others?
2. Read Psalms 15 and 24. Scholars call these the entrance
   liturgies, believing they were chanted by pilgrims enter-
   ing the temple precinct. These psalms ask who can be
   admitted to worship. What does it take to be admitted to
   worship in your congregation? Read Isaiah 56:3-8. Here
   we see how those normally not allowed into the community
   are welcomed. When have you reached out to make someone who is different comfortable in your congregation?
3. Imagine a world populated only by people of your race
   and your culture. Keep a running list this week of things
   you would miss from other cultures, such as food, music,

stories, worship, and friends. What do you think it means if you cannot think of anything you would miss?

4. Say or sing the words to "Guide my feet" as part of your personal meditation. This spiritual asks for God's guidance. Pray that God will guide you.

Understanding

A commonly held stereotype in the early twentieth century was that the prevalence of disease among African Americans was evidence of genetic inferiority. In 1932 the U.S. government identified Macon County, Alabama, as a place where there was a high incidence of syphilis among blacks and funded a large treatment of the disease and a study of their hypothesis. When funds dried up during the Depression, the study changed, unbeknownst to the patients, to an examination of untreated syphilis in the Negro male. For nearly forty years, four hundred men were denied simple antibiotic treatment for a curable disease in order to observe the course of the disease from early stages to death.

Originally 412 men were enrolled in the study. By 1956, 360 men remained. By 1972, only 127 men survived. When the United States Senate uncovered the research, which had been carried along for many years without oversight, they quickly administered treatment to survivors, but it was not until 1991 that President Clinton offered an apology to the men and families of the "Tuskegee Study."

The suffering was tremendous and the assumption that black men were as expendable as laboratory rats was hideous. The sacrifice is made even more meaningless knowing that studies on untreated syphilis had already been done in Norway by the time the Tuskegee Study got underway. Syphilis was known all over the world among many races and ethnicities. There was no reason except racism to study the effects in black men. Despite financial reparations to survivors and heirs, the cost of the Tuskegee Study is inestimable. The price was paid in human lives and added to the astronomical tally of human and financial expenses of racism and discrimination.

The Cost of Racism

If slave labor had not built the pyramids or lofty cathedrals of Europe or commerce in the American South, these things would never have happened. But knowing the human and social cost of slavery and discrimination now, we must question whether anything, anything at all, is worth the cost in lives and spirits.

One of the most costly institutions financially for America was, and is, segregation. In the South, two sets of public restrooms and two different water fountains, one labeled "Whites Only" and the other "Colored," could double the cost of construction. Two separate school systems and two college systems literally cost the society more money than simple integration.

Truthfully, there was a profit to be made in segregation. The substandard "colored" school system saved society money in education because far less money per child was spent to educate minority children. In Texas "Mexican schools" cost the state less money than an integrated school system where the same amount of money would have had to have been spent on white children and Mexican children alike. As it was, substandard Mexican schools represented a savings overall.

Or, take for example, the group of Christian Anabaptists who opposed slavery and moved into South Carolina around 1700 to show that they could carve out a productive plantation without slave labor. Alienated from their slave-owning white neighbors and unable to compete without the labor of slaves, the experiment failed and the Anabaptists returned to the North. Those who became wealthy off their plantations were those who could afford to buy and support slave labor. Not only could they afford the labor, it made them fabulously rich.

Today there are those who profit from other substandard services to minorities, like grocery store owners. Cities have countless grocery stores that charge more for inferior produce, especially in low income, racially mixed neighborhoods. Even today in Austin, Texas, where we live, there are only a few large grocery stores in East Austin (the low economic area of the city). Families are forced to shop at high priced convenience stores because of their close proximity. In more affluent areas of the city, there are fewer "convenience" stores and far more large grocery stores with low prices based on volume. Moreover, convenience store owners are not always local entrepreneurs, but outsiders who take advantage of the poor. They profit from segregation, while the larger community pays the cost.

Overall, the cost of racism to our society has been high. Every undereducated child and every unskilled, unemployed worker contributes less to our society. Educated children, whether minorities or not, generally contribute more to society. Every worker, at every skill level, contributes to the economy, while those without education and training often become dependent on subsidy and a cost to society as a whole.

The Cultural Cost

In addition to the crass financial cost of racism, there are other costs. For example, as a society we've paid a terrible price by dismissing the creative ideas, new concepts, and important opinions of people of color. We have sacrificed valuable human resources because minority people have been excluded from corporations, education, media, and business. Perhaps this is the greatest loss of all. It is a human loss. The talents and gifts of many minority people have been lost, never to be recovered. How many more new inventions, new ways of doing things, new theories will be found in a society that respects the integrity and abilities of people of all races!

The Cost of Racism in Church

Christians have lost credibility as moral leaders in a society where the military succeeds best at cultural diversity and the church models polite segregation. How did we get to this place with things in this order? In all honesty, has it ever been any other way? Many denominations were segregated through the nineteenth century. Not only did Presbyterians and Baptists split black and white. They split north and south, incurring great costs for leadership and facilities for four denominations instead of two.

Even the Church of the Brethren, who opposed slavery and prohibited members from owning slaves, was in reality segregated. Mattie Cunningham Dolby, a bright young Church of the Brethren missionary, a college graduate, and one of the first women to be installed as a minister of a congregation in 1911, nonetheless was asked to leave a congregation in 1924 for reasons of prejudice, according to her children. Customarily, Brethren attend the congregation closest to their homes. New leadership in the congregation Mattie attended counseled her to seek membership in a congregation closer to home. It was a thinly veiled directive to worship with other Negroes in their own congregation, which did not exist within easy travel distance. Her leadership was lost to the Church of the Brethren, a gain for the Methodists and Church of God that she served subsequently.

Brethren also have practiced the holy kiss in worship and at love feast. A query came to the Annual Meeting in the mid-1800s asking whether white Brethren were required to greet black Brethren with the holy kiss. The response of the delegates at the meeting was that it was entirely appropriate for the races to greet each other in the traditional way, with a kiss, but that Brethren should forebear white brothers and sisters who were not ready to kiss their black brethren, knowing that a disingenuous kiss was not given with the proper sentiment. Prejudice cost Brethren real unity.

What Price Membership?

The sacrifice of talented people and people with varieties of gifts for God has always been a problem in the faith community. When the Jews returned to the promised land after exile in Babylon five hundred years before Christ, they looked for ways to revive their culture, a culture that had been decimated by captivity, migration, and intermarriage. In an effort to recover the faith, the priest Ezra denounced marriages between Israelites and foreign women, forcing couples to divorce and foreign wives to go home. Jews in Jesus' time lived under Roman occupation that was hostile to Judaism. Like their ancestors who rebuilt the faith after exile, Pharisees were deeply worried about the possible annihilation of their faith, which explains why they worked so hard to maintain the law and a pure faith.

But overall the good news of both Old and New Testaments is that God offers salvation to all the nations. "I am coming to gather all nations and tongues; and they shall come and shall see my glory" (Isa. 66:18). In Psalms 15 and 24, sometimes called the entrance psalms, the psalmist lays out criteria for admittance to worship. None of the requirements have racial or economic connotations. There are no requirements for belonging based on physical attributes or class or social connections. The only way to belong to the family of God is to believe. Again, Isaiah 56:3-8 describes typical outsiders, like the foreigner and the eunuch, as part of the community, if they believe.

If Judaism could admit that level of cultural diversity, it is no surprise that Paul also opens the church wide to diversity. When Paul found members of the early Corinthian church arguing over who was acceptable and who was not, he admonished the congregation in a letter to appreciate the gifts, graces, and talents of every Christian. He used the famous image of the one body with many members to remind us that every single member enriches the whole community of faith with diversity.

In the body of Christ, differences such as social status, religious style preference, gender, and race no longer exist. In fact, the body cannot function without the different members. One of the costs of racism is the loss of the gifts, graces, and talents of brothers and sisters of various races.

Paul notes what a loss it would be if the body, being all eyes, had no hearing, or being all ears, had no way to smell. Moreover, the weaker or "lesser" members are the ones we are to hold up as truly indispensable. "Our more respectable members do not need this," he says (1 Cor. 12:24). Each person has unique gifts and talents. Each has a function and these functions are not the same or interchangeable or even equal, but they are all valuable. If it is true that not all members of the body can be ears and eyes, then it is also true that the Christian community cannot be made up of people who are all alike. The church needs the diversity of many members in one body.

Paul is specific about the Christian community. Each member is interdependent. Those who have the gift of prophecy cannot say that they have no need of those with the gift of tongues. Paul reminds us that even the members who might be perceived as having the lowest status are given special honor by God's special attention. Therefore, all the members of the body of Christ should never be divided and all should care for each other. After all, it is clear, according to Paul, that God is the source of the wonderful diversity of members and gifts. Therefore, the Christian community can only be enriched with the gifts, graces, and talents of the multiracial and multiethnic members of the church.

The church has the opportunity to be a wonderful model of how cultures and societies can blossom with the inclusion of all people. This inclusiveness would no doubt be a positive and enriching experience. However, it would also mean change, including changes in worship style, music, social activities, and much more. Perhaps the most difficult changes would involve the ways people share power and make decisions in church. These kinds of changes are difficult because they mean changing the patterns of generations. Churches tend to be places of comfort where we enjoy traditions and patterns of the past. In order to make our churches the integrated and diverse places that God wants them to be, we have to modify the structure and worship style of the congregation so as to include all the people of God's interracial family.

It will help us to think of the biblical tradition as a tradition of inclusion and diversity instead of a tradition of sameness and uniformity. From the motley group that fled Egypt and set up camp in the wilderness to the converts from every nation at Pentecost who spoke every language and still understood each other, the family of God is rich because it is diverse. When the church discriminates on account of race, we have robbed God and ourselves of a fortune.

Discussion and Action

1. How integrated or segregated is your community? If segregated, what costs and profits can you associate with

living separately? Are there costs and profits related to integration? What are they? How are they different from the costs and profits of segregation?

2. Look through the worship bulletins from the last five or six worship services at your church. Make a list of the hymns sung. Do they come from a variety of races, cultures, and languages? Does your hymnal or songbook have a selection of hymns from other cultures? Would a person of another culture visiting your church find something familiar in your hymnal? What kind of music has your own culture contributed to church music?

3. Consider going as a group to visit a church whose members are different ethnically from your own. Afterward talk about the style of worship. How did worship reflect the ethnic background of church members? Did you enter with a stereotype of what the worship would be like? How did the worship fulfill or defy your stereotype? How was worship different from your own? How was the music the same or different? What parts of the worship would you adopt to enrich your own worship? Which aspects are unfamiliar or even make you feel uncomfortable? Why?

4. Plan an exchange between your congregation and an ethnic congregation. Exchange preachers or choirs for a Sunday. Encourage the congregations to eat together at a potluck meal. Share personal stories and church histories. How might this relationship become an ongoing aspect of congregational life?

5. Invite a guest from a minority business association to share about challenges and opportunities for minority business owners in your community, or invite a guest from the school system or university to talk about the obstacles concerning race that still face our educational institutions.

6. Talk about what can be done to expand your church's outreach ministries to other racial groups. What services can be provided? What would need to be changed

to attract people of other racial groups? What could be done to make all racial groups feel at home?

7. Expand your views by reading a book by a contemporary ethnic writer. Some examples might include: *Bless Me, Ultima* by Rudolfo Anaya, a story of a young Mexican American boy coming of age in New Mexico; *The Bluest Eye* by Toni Morrison, a book about a little black girl who wishes for blue eyes; or *Farewell to Manzanar* by Jeanne Wakatsuki Houston and James D. Houston.

8. Close by singing together "Guide my feet."

7

Our Struggle with Racism
Romans 7

Racism and prejudice are sins that control our lives. Paul understood how sin can control our lives and explains how Christ gives us freedom from the slavery of sin. Every Christian struggles with the sin of prejudice. As Christians we can have the courage to confront sin and help create the interracial family of God.

Personal Preparation

1. Read Romans 7. What good thing would you like to do that you have trouble accomplishing? What could you be doing to counter racism, but find difficult to do?
2. Paul says that sin controls our lives. What kind of hold does the sin of racism have over your life?
3. Reflect on your own attitudes and prejudices. What attitudes were you raised with? How have they changed over the years?
4. Read Psalm 51 on page 97 in Suggestions for Sharing and Prayer. This is a psalm asking God to remove each one's sin. The first step in removing sin from our lives is to admit our sins and ask God to cleanse us from our sin. Then look at the words to the hymn "There is a balm in Gilead." This spiritual is an appeal for healing. Pray for healing.

Understanding

Gregory Williams was born to a white mother and a father from a mixed-race family. In his early life, the family lived as a white family "of Italian extraction," their mother claimed; but when Greg's mother left their abusive father, Greg and his brother, Mike, went to live among their father's relatives in a black neighborhood of Muncie, Indiana. In his book, *Life on the Color Line,* Greg Williams describes how he learned about his background and about the realities of life for different races. His father chose to tell the two little boys about their relatives as they were traveling to their new home in Indiana. "Remember Miss Sallie who used to work for us in the tavern? . . . It's hard to tell you boys this, but she's really my momma. That means she's your grandmother."

"But that can't be, Dad!" Greg said. "She's colored!"

"That's right, Billy," he continued. "She's colored. That makes you part colored, too."

Greg was overwhelmed by his discovery. "Goose bumps covered my arms as I realized that whatever he was, I was." His little brother began whimpering, saying, "I don't wanta be colored. I don't wanta be colored. We can't go swimmin' or skatin'."

Greg Williams says, "I guess there has never been a time in my life that I haven't been right on the color line." He recalls an incident during segregation in which he was allowed to stay in the "Whites Only" waiting room of the bus station, but his father and caretaker were forced to move to a "Colored" waiting room. On the other hand, he tells how he was passed over for an award at school because awards weren't given to black children. He got out of a scrape with police because he was white, but his girlfriend's white family forbid her to see him because he was black.

His father finally said to him, "Boy, you got a choice. Take it, and get . . . outta here!" Being of both worlds and accepted fully in neither, Greg Williams knew both the advantages of white privilege and the pain of discrimination. The choice for one didn't seem so clear to him as it did to his father. To choose the white world as a way out of poverty and discrimination felt to him like a rejection of the community that took him in and loved him when he was an abandoned little boy. And he clearly didn't want to think of himself as white if being white meant being a racist. Over and over he said, "I ain't white. I don't want to be white." Life became for him a challenge of getting out of poverty without falling into a culture of racism against others.

Facing into Our Own Racism

Few people have the chance to experience racism from both sides, as Greg Williams did. Seeing it from one side is enough, more than enough, but often, the discrimination that is so apparent to the oppressed is practically invisible to the one who discriminates. We don't see ourselves as part of a larger system of racism. We've never discriminated against someone personally, so we're not responsible. It's not apparent to us that our homogeneous communities are that way because people who are different are not really welcomed. It doesn't register that all the opportunities in the world are not available to most people.

Recently, a close friend was telling me about a great job opportunity her son had discovered. The employer was paying a great wage for flexible hours for her son to run errands for him. It seemed to be the perfect job for a student! This employer even needed others to do similar work. I recommended my son, also a student. When my friend told her son that my Derek would be interested in a job, her son was stunned. It seemed that he immediately knew that his employer would never consider hiring my son because he is black.

She called to tell me how sorry she was. I responded by saying that unfortunately this was the way the world was and it was something our family deals with all the time. After I hung up the phone, I could not help but think about our conversation. Did my friend really understand that her children have privileges that my children will never have? They have opportunities that have nothing to do with ability, talent, education, or hard work. These opportunities are the result of their race. My children have few opportunities and it is the result of their race.

Then I wondered, how does she feel about her son working for someone who is racist? Does it bother her son? His reaction suggested that he was well aware of how racist his employer was; so I wondered why he was still willing to work for this man. Was racism something they, as white people, could generally forget about? My family did not have the luxury. My friend and her family are not racists, but they live fairly comfortably in a world of racism. They enjoy the privileges of being white, without even thinking of these benefits as "privileges."

There are those who believe that racism no longer exists and that all people have equal opportunity. But the experience of people of color is that almost daily there are obstacles still to be overcome. It takes careful looking sometimes to see the racism and then take action to counter it. For instance, how many of us shop at stores that have many low paid employees from minority groups, but no managers or supervisors who are minorities? How often do we listen to racist jokes or comments, but only silently think to ourselves how inappropriate or offensive the comments and jokes are?

As Christians we struggle with our own prejudice. Each of us has stereotypes that we were taught as children. Fears that we carry consciously or sometimes even unconsciously may lead us to unfair judgments about people because of race or ethnic background. Perhaps in our own honesty, we know that we too hold beliefs and prejudice that are unfair and hateful. My mother can tell stories not only about others, but about herself and the attitudes as a white person that she learned as a child growing up in Oklahoma. She was shocked to find herself in integrated schools when her family moved to Kansas in the 1940s. For years those attitudes and suspicions stayed with her and were obstacles to enjoying the friendship and cultures of minority peoples.

Recognizing Sin

Why is there such nonchalance about racism when Christians are otherwise very concerned for justice in the world? Is it, as it seems Paul is saying in Romans 7, just plain difficult to do the good we say we want to do? Is it that we were just born sinners and unable to ever hope to overcome sin, so why try?

Paul understood well what it meant to have sin control his life. In Romans 7, he writes about the hold that sin had over him. "I do not understand my own actions. For I do not do what I want, but I do the very thing I hate" (Rom. 7:15). He struggled with the difference between what he knew was good and his own sinful actions. "For I do not do the good I want, but the evil I do not want is what I do. Now if I do what I do not want, it is no longer I that do it, but sin that dwells within me" (Rom. 7:19-20). Paul writes persuasively that we are ever at war with sin, in this case the sin of racism.

As Christians we also proclaim that there is power greater than sin and something more powerful than death. But Paul notes in this passage that even though we think we are living faithfully, if we allow a sin like racism to exist, all our good intentions turn to nothing. Faithful living in the presence of sin only corrupts faithfulness or the law.

Take for example the Supreme Court debate on state laws that kept the races "separate but equal." States claimed that they could uphold the law of equality for the races and still keep races segregated. If Paul had been a trial lawyer, he might have said that the law of equality, while good and Godly, was corrupted by the presence of the sin of segregation. In reality, everything was separate and nothing was equal, not schools, not community services, and not the justice system itself. Segregation was the sin that corrupted the law of equality. The Supreme Court struck down the concept of "separate but equal" as unconstitutional.

If a sin has corrupted our faithfulness, the good things we want to do come to nothing. We cannot at the same time be against racism in our personal lives and allow racism to flourish elsewhere. If we do, our claim that we are not racist comes to nothing. When Christians carry out the letter of the law, believing that they alone can achieve goodness, the only thing they produce is arrogance. In the words of poet T. S. Eliot, they do "the right thing for the wrong reason."

Paul is saying more than it's difficult to do the right thing at times. He's saying that doing the right thing is not always the right thing to do. When we claim that we are not racist yet tolerate discrimination in others or use privileges others don't have or fail to challenge racism in our communities, nothing good comes of our claims that we are just. Of course, no one person is responsible for all racism. No one person can singlehandedly do away with it. It is not an option for many people to move into integrated communities or create integrated work places. But it is possible for everyone to make their community a welcoming place. Everyone can reject racist jokes or comments. Everyone can challenge racist hiring practices. Everyone can take business to stores and hotels and restaurants that are fair employers. Everyone who has privileges can share them. Everyone can insist on good education for all children. Only when we do these things will our claim to fairness be real.

White Privilege

Perhaps one of the greatest obstacles to overcoming racism is what is called white privilege. Good education, job opportunities, political clout, and police protection, to name a few, are so natural that most white people would deny they are "privileges," yet when we look closely at our society, these things are afforded automatically to majority whites, but not so automatically to minorities. They are privileges given on account of race.

For example, my family learned a long time ago that if Kathy, who is white, takes the car to the shop, she is likely to get a lower price for repairs. When renting an apartment, units are much more likely to be available if Kathy makes the first contact. Kathy gets "warning" tickets from the police for speeding. Steve gets a ticket every time he is pulled over.

These privileges seem small, but there are bigger privileges that can make a real difference. Mortgage loans, car loans, and other banking transactions have generally been automatic privileges for white people. Acceptance into private clubs, neighborhood associations, and other organizations is often limited to white people. Though it would be difficult to give up the privileges of association with institutions that discriminate, this is the action we as Christians must take to live out our antiracist views.

Racism, white privilege, and a host of other ways to discriminate are so much a part of our culture and sinful nature that we are always at war with them. It is only by ongoing confession and prayer that each of us can work to free ourselves from this sin. Paul reminds us that it is Jesus Christ who saves us from this slavery to sin and frees us to be children of God. In addition we have to work to correct the sin around us. We must confront the sin inside ourselves and also in others. What should we say? When do we confront someone? What comments go unanswered?

In *Slaves in the Family*, plantation descendent Edward Bell makes a confession:

> The subject of the plantations stirred conflicting emotions. I felt proud (how rare the stories!) and sentimental (how touching the cast of family characters!). At the same time, the slave business was a crime that had not fully been acknowledged. It would be a mistake to say that I felt guilt for the past. A person cannot be culpable for the acts of others, long dead, that he or she could not have influenced. Rather than responsible, I felt accountable for what had happened, called on to try to explain it. I also felt shame about the broken society that had washed up when the tide of slavery receded.
>
> I decided I would make an effort, however inadequate and personal, to face the plantations, to reckon with them rather than ignore their realities or make excuses for them.

Like Ball we all have to come to terms with our part in racism and reckon with it rather than ignore it. Ending the racism and prejudice in our lives and in our world is not a one-time action, but rather a constant battle. Our faith in God can help us confront the sin of racial prejudice in our own lives and give us courage to speak boldly to challenge the sin of racism. Our faith can also give us the insight into our privileges and how we can share those privileges with all people.

Discussion and Action

1. As a group, list all the opportunities you can think of for education, employment, and entertainment for young people in your community. Go back through the list and mark the opportunities that might be limited for a minority person. For instance, would a person of color have a realistic opportunity to date any young person in the community? How would a person of color fare in the job market seeking a management job in your area? Are all real estate and rental properties available to people of color in your community?

2. On the flip side, in what ways do you think whites are privileged in your community?

3. Name some of the good things you would like to do but can't seem to accomplish. If God and your faith are your motivations, what keeps you from doing a good thing? More specifically, what keeps you from challenging racism in your community? If God is not your motivation, what is? What good can come from any other motivation, such as success or money?

4. Reflect on your own attitudes, prejudice, and racism. Confess these to God and ask God for forgiveness. Acknowledge that God loves his interracial family and wants all of his children to love each other.

5. Write a poem, a prayer, or a short meditation that expresses the feelings you have about racism and prejudice. Share your writing with the group if you feel comfortable.

6. Talk about ways that you personally or the covenant group can help increase privileges for all people. Where in your community can you challenge racism? Do it. Contribute financially to a scholarship fund that will increase an underprivileged person's chances for a good education. Give an employee management training. Avoid shopping in businesses with discriminating employment policies and let the business know about your decision.

7. Close by singing "There is a balm in Gilead."

8

Racism in the Church
1 Corinthians 11:17-34

We would all like to believe that the church is a place unscathed by the sin of racism. However, the church is made up of human beings who bring to it all their fears and prejudices. Historically, racism has divided the church and even unified it at times.

Personal Preparation

1. Read 1 Corinthians 11:17-34. Paul writes to the church in Corinth about the division taking place in the community. In what ways is your church community divided? Where are you in the divisions?

2. When you take part in the Lord's Supper, how important is it for you to be unified with others? What can you do to be unified with others?

3. How well are you unified at church with people of other races? How could you better get to know people different from you racially or culturally at church or in your denomination?

4. Read Psalm 41, a wisdom psalm with elements of a lament. Notice that, like a wisdom psalm, it begins with a proverb ("happy are those..."). Then it shifts to lament language of conflict and constraint. Even the close friend rejects the psalmist. Read the psalm again, thinking of "I" as the church and the "sin" as racism. Read for the teaching and the conviction in this psalm.

5. Read or sing the hymn "I want Jesus to walk with me." This spiritual is an appeal for God to stay with us no matter what our situation. Pray for God's continued presence in your life and in the lives of others.

Understanding

In his epic novel *Hawaii*, James Michener tells a fictional story, but it effectively represents the racist mission philosophy of European and North American Protestantism for many years. After Hawaii had been discovered and exploited by merchants, the church descended on the islands and made converts of the people. As Michener tells his tale, Keoki, a young Hawaiian Christian in the nineteenth century, shows promise as a religious leader among his people. The missionaries from America arrange for him to study in the U.S. at Yale, where he is a very successful student, eagerly awaiting an assignment in his homeland. Though he does well in school and is well respected by others, he is never allowed to be ordained. He pleads with the missionary, saying, "I have proved myself. I proved myself at Yale College, when I stood in the snow begging an education. I proved myself at Cornwall, where I was the top student in the mission school. And here in Lahaina I have protected you against the sailors. What more must I do to prove myself?" The missionary agrees that Keoki is qualified for membership, but not ministry. When his wife asks "Why not?" the missionary answers, "He's a heathen."

As happens in many real life cases, Keoki is stripped of his native religion and brought into the church, but he is never truly accepted there. The church sends a double message: you must be a Christian but you cannot belong to the Christian community as a full member, much less a leader.

This story will ring true for American Indians on the mainland, too. In the late nineteenth and early twentieth centuries, Native American children were systematically separated from families and raised in Indian boarding schools run by the Bureau of Indian Affairs. Like the famous athlete James Thorpe, they were made to speak English and dress in western style clothing.

Over time they were weaned of their native culture and faith, but for all their efforts to conform to American culture, forced though it was, they were not allowed to be part of it either. There was not even a place in the church for them to share their understanding of Christian faith and no positions for them to be leaders in church structures and government.

Missionary efforts have brought many immigrants from many cultures to the Christian faith, but few immigrant or ethnic Christians are integrated into multi-ethnic congregations. So on any given Sunday morning, segregated by language, customs, and prejudice, Korean Americans gather in Korean churches, Hispanic Americans gather in Hispanic churches, African Americans go to church with African Americans. And, by and large, Anglo Christians gather for church with Anglos. Why has the church, the very institution that proclaims God's love for all people and insists on unity, done so poorly at overcoming prejudice, discrimination, and racism?

Sacred Segregation

Racism in the church has a long legacy, one that reaches hundreds of years back into church history, for example, the conquistadors' view of peoples in the Americas as subhuman, the murderous crusades against Muslims in the Middle East, and mission efforts in Africa and Asia that viewed the native peoples as inferior and in need of saving (but not empowering). The period before and during the Civil War was a critical time in U.S. history, when race discrimination developed in the church. Even the denominations that had a unified and clear position against slavery experienced tensions over the practice of slavery, and people lined up along doctrinal lines on the issue.

The Brethren, a small sect of pacifistic pietists and Anabaptists, made it clear as early as 1782 that no members should purchase or keep Africans as slaves. Throughout this pre-Civil War era, the message was unchanging. Even those who inherited slaves were to set those slaves free. The group's Annual Meeting statements admonished church members, saying that justifying slavery publicly or privately was not allowed and disciplinary actions would be taken against a member who upheld the institution of slavery.

In *Racism and the Church*, Brethren writer Shantilal Bhagat reports:

> Long before anyone else, except a few Quakers, was aroused, our Dunker elders were deeply disturbed and persistently vocal against slavery. It was, they said, an unmitigated evil not to be tolerated, much less practiced, by a church member. Moreover, anyone desiring to join the church had first to follow a long list of specific instruction to free all the slaves in the presence of witnesses, providing freedmen with food, clothes, bedding, religious guidance, and other benefits — all to be carried out under the careful supervision of the local church. No minister was permitted even to hold pro-slavery views, and stern disciplinary action was spelled out for treatment of any deviants.

The position of the church exacted a great toll on church members, particularly those living south of the Mason-Dixon Line whose views seemed traitorous to their slaveholding neighbors. Pressures from neighbors and governmental agencies made life difficult for many Brethren Christians. Elder John Kline, a Virginian, was even assassinated in 1864 by Confederate sympathizers who may have believed the church leader was a spy for the North.

At times the liberal policies of the church were ambiguous for black Brethren. Samuel Weir gained his freedom when his owner wished to become a member of a Brethren congregation. To comply with the decisions of the church, Andrew McClure freed his slaves, including Weir who had been with him for nearly twenty years. After he was manumitted, Weir also joined the church and, with the help of other Brethren, moved to Ohio to live with a white family there. Weir learned to read and write and later studied with a black Baptist minister, but he was denied admission to Brethren fellowships in the county where he lived. When churches in another county accepted him and licensed him to ministry, he was limited to ministry to other blacks. Despite the church's prejudices, Weir gave his house and the lot to the church to be used for ministry to blacks.

Though the Brethren were segregated in many cases, they never split into two denominations as other Protestant groups did. Several denominations split over the issue of slavery decades before the Civil War, and some remain separated to this day. Others, though reunified, have had difficulty overcoming their history of division.

While the Church of the Brethren remained unified against slavery, it was generally silent on issues of race for the next hundred years. As in the case of Samuel Weir, Brethren and other Protestant denominations in the North took a firm stand against slavery, but few churches became integrated. African Americans were often not allowed to have membership in churches, or were at least discouraged from it. It was during the Civil War era, and in response to it, that the traditional African American denominations (African Methodist Episcopal, African Methodist Episcopal Zion, and others) were founded. They welcomed blacks when few churches encouraged or reached out to the newly freed slaves.

Churches have continued to develop along the lines of race and ethnic background, resulting in a very segregated Sunday morning hour. Reaching out to people of other races and ethnic backgrounds has been minimal and halfhearted. Few churches yet reflect the racial diversity of the interracial family of God.

Part of the problem is that congregations exist in homogeneous neighborhoods where ethnic diversity does not exist. That in itself is a sign of racial segregation. In some cases, language barriers keep Christians segregated. In other cases, traditions are deeply rooted. The prospect of learning new and strange sounding music or prayer or theology is unappealing to the dominant group. Acquiring new forms of worship, new ideas, and new members takes deliberate effort and requires strong leadership, for the forces of inertia, habit, and prejudice are great.

Not a New Problem

Division in the church is nothing new in the church's history. According to Paul's writings in 1 Corinthians, the church of Corinth dealt with a great controversy, particularly regarding the Lord's Supper. Apparently when the congregation gathered for a fellowship meal, those who arrived early ate the meal instead of waiting for others. The consequence was that latecomers remained hungry and others drank too much wine.

For Paul, the meal eaten together was an essential part of the Eucharistic celebration. The breaking of bread and the sharing of the cup marked the beginning and end of the meal that is celebrated in remembrance of Jesus. A Christian leaves behind his or her individualistic self to join the community in this important action. The body unified in the celebration of the agape meal represents the very unity of Christ.

Paul was concerned about the inequities in the Corinthian church and believed that there would be serious consequences. He gave the church a warning about the coming judgment and lectured them about the meaning of the Lord's Supper. At the occasion of the agape meal, the body of Christ must overcome its divisions and find unity. If the meal is causing division, then it must be dispensed with to achieve the unity of the body of Christ. More than the meal, it is important to preserve the ritual exchange of bread and wine as a symbol of unity.

For Christians, the bonds of fellowship should extend beyond the divisions of class and race and ethnic background. Yet, many churches and denominations have difficulty bringing people together across racial lines. Even leadership positions of integrated denominations and congregations generally do not reflect the racial makeup of the members. To overcome institutional racism, it takes a continued commitment to make leadership truly representative of *all* the people.

Paul reminds us that when we embrace the diverse family of God, we reflect the unity that we have in Christ. In every aspect of our lives as disciples of Christ we are called to reach out to others, actively pursuing reconciliation between all members, especially across color lines, so that we truly reflect God's interracial family.

Christians have paid a high price to remain in their own racial and ethnic groupings on Sunday morning. For many years, the vast resources of African American music and spirituals have been absent in white churches, as have the contributions of Asian Americans, Hispanics and other people of color. It is not easy to make our denominations and churches multiracial. It *is* easy to make excuses like "African Americans don't like to serve on committees" or "Asians are not interested in our church," but we must make every effort to make our churches welcoming to all people.

Surely the message of the gospel is one of reconciliation. True reconciliation in the church means that all people will be welcomed as brothers and sisters in Christ. It means that no one group controls power and privilege. It means sharing responsibility and welcoming new ideas. It means reaching out to our neighbors in new ways. All of this can happen if we truly repent of the sin of racism and take concrete action to make our churches representative of the interracial family of God.

Some of the most heartbreaking violent conflicts in our world are those between Christians of different racial, religious, or ethnic backgrounds. Northern Ireland, torn between Protestants and Catholics, and the Balkans, ripped apart by ethnic cleansing, must make Christ weep. Instead of caring for Christ's way in the world, we all too often care only about "our" way. Christian love, to be genuine, must extend beyond the comfortable groups of like-looking and like-minded people to include all people.

Paul recognized that the Christian community could not ultimately withstand the division that tore apart the church in Corinth. We too must repent and commit ourselves to action that heals divisions and rejoices in reconciliation of the family of God.

Discussion and Action

1. Why do you personally think the Sunday morning hour is the most racially segregated hour of the week?
2. In what ways, if any, does your congregation send a double message to people who are different, i.e., "Please join us, but do everything according to our tradition."

3. Make a top-ten list of "Reasons We Avoid Mixing Races and Cultures in Our Congregation." Go back over the list and talk about how to overcome each barrier on the list.

4. In your mind, what are the gains and losses of isolating ourselves racially and ethnically on Sunday morning?

5. To what extent is the Lord's Supper a personal experience for you, and to what extent is it a community experience? How does discord in the congregation affect the way you experience communion or the agape meal? And to what extent is racism or prejudice the source of discord?

6. Especially if you have no racial variety in your congregation, how would you describe your congregation's level of racism?

7. Cultures affect worship styles. Plan to visit a congregation that is racially different. What similarities can you find between your congregation's worship and another's? What keeps people from worshiping together? What advantages are there to worshiping together?

8. Ask someone who has lived in another culture, either within the United States or in another country, to describe their worship style and how the culture affected congregational life.

9. Close by singing together "I want Jesus to walk with me." Pray that your congregation will grow to understand that God wants harmony among all the races of the world and that God wants us to work to establish the interracial family of God.

9

Challenging Racism
Amos 5:14-15, 21-25; Acts 2

Naturally, Christians must challenge racism. But the prophet Amos warns the faithful that their motivations for doing so are very important. God listens to sincere pleas on behalf of the oppressed, but God despises the false piety that challenges an evil in order to make the oppressor look better. When we challenge racism, we pray for the right spirit, the spirit of justice over self-preservation.

Personal Preparation

1. Read Amos 5. How do you practice repentance in your life? How, if at all, has repenting led you to change your life?
2. Read Acts 2:1-13. How do you suppose people understood each other though they spoke different languages? What basic Christian truths do all Christians understand in every language and every culture?
3. What do you think will happen ultimately if the church does not challenge the problem of racism? How do you think God will judge the church on the issue of racism?
4. The spiritual "Wade in the water" is a hymn of encouragement and hope. It challenges us to go forth with courage and trust in God's actions. Sing or read the words to this hymn. Pray that God will give you courage to do what is right and just.

Understanding

Martin Luther King, Jr., did not plan to be a civil rights activist.
He was an up-and-coming pastor in Montgomery, Alabama, with
a new Ph.D. in hand. He had a wife and a child and a new baby
about to be born. He grew up in the segregated South and had his
share of experiences with racism, but Martin Luther King, Jr.,
had long since committed himself to ministry. Then Rosa Parks
set off the Montgomery bus boycott by refusing to move to the
back of the bus where Negroes were supposed to sit to leave seats
in the front for white passengers. When she was arrested, King
and other Montgomery black leaders went to work quickly. Their
response was to plan a day of boycotting the local bus system,
which was used largely by blacks. By refusing to ride the buses
for one day, they would send a message to local government that
they had economic power to demand equality. King had his doubts
about whether blacks in Montgomery could manage without the
bus system, but when he watched the earliest bus pull up at the
stop in front of his house that Monday morning, the only occu-
pant was the driver!

The day of boycotting was more successful than anyone imag-
ined, which left black leaders suddenly wondering whether they
should continue the boycott until the bus system was integrated,
or consider it a success after one day. They met at Ralph
Abernathy's church to evaluate the action and decided then and
there to organize the Montgomery Improvement Association to
address problems of racism and inequality in the city. King was
unanimously elected president. A half hour later he met with a
throng of several thousand people who resolved with him to let
the boycott go on, which it did—for 281 days—until the courts
ordered the buses to be integrated.

At her trial Rosa Parks told the judge that she refused to move
to the back of the bus because she was tired. And King told re-
porters, "We're all tired. Mrs. Rosa Parks speaks for us all." People
had reached a point of weariness with injustice. They were tired
of the unfairness and violence that victimized them. And when
they couldn't stand the injustice any longer, life changed. It
changed dramatically for Martin Luther King, Jr., who was

propelled into leadership when people needed it, when there wasn't any way to hold back the tide of justice any more.

Some whites were changed by the brutality and inequality they saw against minorities. In a show of penitence and solidarity, white college students enrolled in all-black colleges and participated in the nonviolent actions to integrate lunch counters in the South. Now, in reviews of the twentieth century, the famous pictures of Paul Laprad, a white student from Indiana, surface again showing Laprad being dragged backward from his stool at a lunch counter in Nashville, Tennessee, and beaten by angry, racist whites. Laprad was arrested and tried. Though officers testified that students were sitting quietly at the lunch counters, the judge returned a guilty verdict.

Waves of students sat at the lunch counter that day and were arrested, one after another. As they streamed into the jail, the first protesters were there to welcome new ones with singing and hugging. Laprad said, "It reminded me of how I think some of the New Testament Christians must have gone to jail." Like Paul and Silas reasoned in Acts 16, if justice is illegal, then the only appropriate place for a Christian is in jail. Paul and Silas had a chance to escape, but didn't take it. Even when they were told that authorities would permit them to leave, they refused. Paul wanted to expose the scandal of injustice that city officials of Philippi had committed. There was no better way than to speak from jail.

Let Justice Roll

In the time of the prophet Amos, not long before the exile in Babylon, Israel was wracked by injustice and inequality for the poor. Some Israelites had gotten rich off the labor of the poor, and they gloated about their successes. They never lifted a finger to help the less fortunate brother or sister in the family of God, but they continued to make the required ritual sacrifices and burnt offerings to please God. To these people Amos relays God's utter wrath and threatens judgment for them.

When the prophet Amos confronts the children of Israel, he reminds them that if they repent of their sin and turn around, they can once again find favor with God. "Seek good and not evil, that

you may live" (5:14). You who hate the poor and love your ex-
travagant life styles, he says, love what you hate and hate what
you love. In other words, hate the injustice that you have loved so
long and love the poor whom you have hated. This is the only
way to be reconciled to God.

Justice and equality for the poor in Israel were not options, just
as they were not options for the people of Montgomery in 1956
and Nashville in 1959. There comes a time when justice will as-
sert itself. The reticence of whites to integrate and protect the
rights of blacks would eventually have consequences, potentially
disastrous ones. Things were at a breaking point in April of 1959
when Charles Mack Parker, a black man, was dragged from jail
and lynched by a mob in Poplarville, Mississippi. Famous Southern novelist William Faulkner pleaded for calm and cautioned
blacks to "go slow now" in an article in *Look* magazine. W. E. B.
DuBois challenged Faulkner to a debate on this very topic: whether
the struggle for justice should unfold slowly or in a hurry, whether
blacks could have justice immediately, or whether whites should
be let down easily and protected from the jolt of justice.

Amos had no tolerance for the complacency of the rich and
their patience for slow change. His instruction to "hate evil and
love good, and establish justice in the gate" says nothing about
softening the blow or easing into a new situation. If there is an
injustice, penance must be done or people must face the consequences. In the face of ongoing evil, the NRSV says God will "let
justice roll down like waters, and righteousness like an everflowing
stream." But the King James Version of the Bible translates Amos
5:24 in a more powerful way. It says God will "let *judgment* roll
down like water." The same term that we often naively translate
as "justice" is the same term that can be just as easily translated
"judgment." The choice of translations gives the passage two completely different meanings. But the more likely meaning is that
God will punish injustice relentlessly and will not be gracious
when people knowingly sin against others and do not challenge
injustice. God has given us the work of social justice to do. If we
do not do it, God will let judgment roll down on us. Judgment is
God's work to do.

To use Amos 5 in our own age, we have to transform the language of scripture to apply to issues facing people of faith today, in this case to race discrimination. Amos directs his venom against economic injustice, but he could just as easily be speaking of racism. This passage speaks broadly to injustice. As with many issues, a privileged class of people is exploiting people without privilege. And the King James Version, which accents that scary word *judgment*, is even more direct because it reminds most of us of our complicity in injustice and how painful but necessary it is to relinquish the privileges that we have grown up with.

Amos is not without hope for sinners who repent. Those who are ready to accept the challenges of a new life of faith and justice may escape damning judgment. However, Amos is not so interested in helping the sinner escape judgment as he is in protecting those who are endangered in society. In his day the Israelite monarchy made many social changes that were bad news for the poor. Amos, like Archbishop Romero, the Salvadoran bishop who lived and worked among the poor, spent his time advocating for the poor, not holding the hands of the wealthy who were going to have to face real change in their lives or live with the consequences. He, like Martin Luther King, Jr., focused on the needs of the oppressed and not on his own piety, though his defense of the poor turns out to be the best piety. And like the white students who went to school with black college students and sat at lunch counters with them until they were beaten and arrested, Amos sets the example by leaving his comfortable life as a shepherd and dresser of sycamore trees to speak and live the truth.

Despite his disdain for wretched sinners, Amos gives over a great deal of his prophecy to them in the form of warnings to repent, to change the status quo, to challenge injustice and inequality, or be prepared to suffer God's judgment. He may care for the oppressed, but he apparently cares about Israel, too, enough to implore them to change before it's too late.

How About a Melting Pot?

If scripture calls us to challenge inequalities, what should we be challenging people to become? It's not enough to demand that people stop behaving a certain way without suggesting the way they should be behaving. For years Americans have described the country as a melting pot, a place where color and culture do not matter. Does scripture say that there are no real differences in the family of God or that the way to deal with differences is to ignore them? Should we hold up as our goal the great American melting pot in which races and cultures lose their distinctiveness, one culture being indistinguishable from another?

Often passages such as Galatians 3 have been used to buttress the "melting pot" notion of the nation and the church. But the Acts 2 account of the people speaking many tongues at Pentecost gives a much different understanding. Acts 2:7 does not describe God's family as a group without unique differences. At no time are they described as even a people of "one language." The people of the Pentecost hear each one "speaking in the native tongue of each." They are more like a rainbow where each color is distinct than a melting pot, where individual distinctions are lost.

Acts describes a vibrant church that speaks many languages. We are today a church that speaks French, Spanish, Tagalog, Creole, German, English, and many more. As we have seen in earlier lessons, language and even food can become points of division and matters of cultural and racial privilege. But the visions of Amos and Acts are that God and the Holy Spirit draw together a church, an interracial church, where every language and culture are present, but in which no language or culture is privileged.

Where Amos's wake-up call is blunt and hard hitting, the psalmist reassures us that God desires us to change, and change will have its own rewards. Psalm 85 is a "restoration" psalm. It is a prayer for the restoration of God's favor. The word *restore* in the psalm is the same as the word for "repent" in Hebrew. We repent and God restores us to wholeness. The restoration that the psalmist describes comes, however, at some cost. Scholars often associate Psalm 85 with Israel after the exile when they have repented and paid dearly for their unfaithfulness by years of forced deportation to a foreign land. Our conversion from a racist world view to a Pentecost world view will be equally expensive and require that dominating groups give up privilege; but like the Israelites, the restoration we will experience when we become the family that God wants us to be is priceless. The struggle, as Amos knew, is in convincing privileged people that restoration is greater than the benefits of wealth.

There are glimpses of repentance in our culture. The government has publicly apologized to the black families of Tuskegee patients who suffered through syphilis experiments and to Japanese Americans who were interned in camps in the U.S. as enemies during World War II. Baptists have apologized to African Americans for their part in the legacy of slavery and segregation in the United States. Korean Americans and African Americans in Los Angeles have worked at healing their racial conflict. And a shift in mission philosophy to embrace other cultures instead of replacing them indicates that repentance is possible.

Penance and Action

After penance comes action to correct the injustices for which we need to repent. It does no good to repent without change. To truly repent of racism and change to become an interracial family of God, the church must be an organization that actively seeks to be antiracist. While it takes energy and hard work to go beyond the boundaries of race, there are wonderful examples of groups of people who have transcended the racism of culture and language to be antiracist. Here are just a few:

> Project HEARTS (Harmony Encourages Awareness, Responsibilities and Togetherness) builds understanding between two Kansas City elementary schools. This project, started in 1989 by teachers at urban E. F. Swinney Magnet School and suburban Red Bridge Elementary School, builds understanding between races. Parents, students, and teachers are all "making a difference" in the world by joint projects, celebrations, and friendships.

> After the 1992 Los Angeles riot, the Study Circles Resource Center began providing adult study circles short readings, questions and prompts, suggestions, and much more to help small groups of adults discuss sensitive topics. Study groups include Asians, African Americans, whites, and other racial

groups. While topics such as race can often cause disagreement and hurt feelings, the study circle format is designed to promote civility. Members share personal experiences and debate broader issues.

A group of Disciples of Christ youth expanded their boundaries and experienced multiculturalism firsthand. Ten Asians, ten black youth, and ten white youth lived together in a retreat setting. This experience was a turning point for the youth who reported they "will never be the same again."

First Church of the Brethren, Chicago, has worked intentionally at being an interracial church. Both white members and African American members with a long history of trying to meet the needs of the local community have committed themselves to building an antiracist church.

These are true acts of repentance in which people turn away from injustice and stand on God's side. It's too bad that in this age of self-actualization and self-centeredness this sort of repentance is out of vogue. We avoid dwelling on sins and guilt that drag us down and make us feel bad about ourselves. It's too bad because without repentance we are like the Israelites who faithfully offered burnt sacrifice but never lived faithfully. It's too bad because, the truth is, real fulfillment comes from understanding ourselves in the scope of God's creation, and that requires repentance or change from seeing ourselves as all-powerful to seeing that God is all-powerful. The good news is that repentance also offers up real liberation. People of faith who repent and give up the injustice of racism and all other injustices have lost nothing and gained everything. They can say without fear, "Let judgment roll down like waters, and righteousness like an everflowing stream."

Discussion and Action

1. As a group talk about what you want to achieve ultimately by challenging racism. What are some of the differences between the melting pot image and the rainbow image? Why are these differences important? Think of other

images that portray a world where there is diversity? Render these images as collages, posters, bumper stickers, or clay sculptures. Display them where you meet regularly as a reminder of the need to challenge racism.

2. In what ways do you as a church or as individuals need to repent? What race prejudices do you need to repent of? Encourage each other with stories of repentance that unburdened you. Also, how did repentance lead to change in your life?

3. All too often we only hear about the racist incidents in our society. Tell about projects and work being done in your community or around the country to combat racism in our culture.

4. As you see it, what kinds of changes will people have to make to overcome racism in your community? What are the benefits of those changes? What privileges will whites and other dominant groups lose in order to have racial justice?

5. List some projects that your church might be able to do as an antiracist church. Some examples might be: sponsor an antiracist speech contest at the local high school or elementary school; give a grant to a local teacher to include multicultural education projects in his/her classroom; find a way to welcome all people of every race who move into your church community; plan joint worship with neighboring congregations of other ethnic groups; raise money to add antiracist children's books and materials in the local public library or school library; prepare a message or article for the church newsletter on what you have learned in this curriculum.

6. Establish an ongoing relationship with people of other races by seeking out a pen pal or by sending e-mail to a friend of another race. Encourage members of your family to do the same. What can you learn from others about their life experience? What might you share about some of the differences in your life experience, your views of

the world, or your culture? Learn firsthand what some of the similarities might be.

7. Assign someone in the group to inform the local school system of resources that teachers might use to teach children and youth to become more aware of racism. For example, suggest that schools subscribe to *Teaching Tolerance,* an educational magazine that is provided free to all teachers from the Southern Poverty Law Center, 400 Washington Avenue, Montgomery, AL 36104.

8. Give each person in your group a hexagon shaped paper. Provide markers, colored pencils, and crayons. Ask each person to make a symbol of their own ethnic, racial background. On a bulletin board or wall, connect the papers to form a quilt or mosaic that represents the group. How are the symbols similar? How do the symbols show diversity? What racial or ethnic groups are missing?

9. Close by singing or reading the words to "Wade in the water" (p. 103) as a prayer. Ask God for the courage and strength to repent and challenge racism in yourself, your community, and your church.

10

Living Beyond Racism
Revelation 21:1-4, 22-25

Scripture presents a vision of a world beyond injustice. The new Jerusalem is a city free of racism, a place of salvation toward which biblical history is moving. It is the city where all are welcomed and where the gates are never shut. Each of us is called to help make this vision a reality in our local communities, our churches, and our nation.

Personal Preparation

1. Read Matthew 20:20-28, Mark 10:35-45, and Luke 22:24-27. In this story, the disciples worry about their power and position in the kingdom. What is your relationship to Jesus? What worries you about your relationship?
2. Read Revelation 21:1-4, 22-25. Think about the previous nine lessons. How have you been affected as a Christian by thinking and studying about racism?
3. Read Psalm 150, a psalm of praise. Also, read or sing the hymn "Beyond the dying sun'" about a hope for a better world. How have you worked in your life to make a better world?

Understanding

In 1942, just months after the Japanese bombed Pearl Harbor, Hawaii, President Roosevelt issued Civilian Exclusion Order No. 27 requiring each American family of Japanese ancestry living in the Western Defense Command of the United States to register with the government and be removed from the West Coast as possible enemies of the state. More than 100,000 Japanese immigrants and Japanese Americans, in whose culture respect for authority is paramount, sold their earthly possessions and with few questions took what they could carry to internment camps in the western United States.

Florence Daté Smith, whose parents were Japanese immigrants and she a U.S. citizen, boarded a bus with her family in California and disembarked at a race track where they would live in horse stalls for several months before being relocated to a camp in desert land in Utah. In all, Florence lived for a year and a half in camps guarded day and night by soldiers and ringed with barbed wire. Her possessions were stolen, her mail censored, and her rights stripped, though charges were never brought against her personally.

How could this have happened? How could the President issue an order against Japanese Americans but not Italian or German Americans whose distant relatives were also U.S. enemies during the war? How could more than 100,000 people (70 percent of them American citizens) be marched off to prison with so little resistance, especially when there were no specific charges against them?

Florence describes her belief as a young school-aged child in a vision of American life. "All through my childhood, my parents encouraged me to integrate American values. I learned them well in public school—the beliefs and concepts of democracy, equality, the Bill of Rights, and the Constitution." It was a vision full of promise and hope for immigrant families who sought a better life in a new land. And though Japanese Americans experienced discrimination, the vision of freedom and equality sustained them until things went terribly wrong.

Faith's Vision

The American dream has failed many people—Native Americans, descendants of slaves, immigrants. It is a dream that functions well for a large and privileged portion of the nation but holds little promise for people of color. The Christian faith also has a vision, one that is based on the inclusive love of God and not on the weak and unreliable ideals of humans. The vision is present in the whole witness of scripture from the Old Testament to the New and in the testament of God's people who are at times the persecuted, the minority, the slaves, the foreigners, and the despised. It is a vision of a world in which God's unending love and patience are the pattern for our relationships with each other in the faith community.

This vision of how the world should be begins with the recognition that God is the Creator of life and the only one worthy of praise. Other than for God, there is no distinction of greatness. Though it comes at the end of the Psalter, Psalm 150 expresses the first and fundamental step of faith: know God and praise God. "Let everything that breathes praise the LORD!" (v. 6). First there is God and then there is everything else. Among breathing, living beings that God created, there is no hierarchy, no privilege, no superiority. There is only a common God of surpassing greatness.

In the Synoptic Gospels, Matthew, Mark, and Luke, the topic of privilege comes up again. In Matthew, the mother of two disciples comes to Jesus and asks Jesus to promise that her sons, the sons of Zebedee, "will sit, one at your right hand and one at your left, in your kingdom" (Matt. 20:21-28). Jesus rejects the request, saying, " . . . to sit at my right hand and at my left, this is not mine to grant, but it is for those for whom is has been prepared by my Father" (20:23). In Luke, Jesus settles a dispute the disciples are having over which one of them is greatest. He answers: "For who is greater, the one who is at the table or the one who serves? Is it not the one at the table? But I am among you as one who serves" (Luke 22:27).

Both stories, in their own ways, contrast the disciples' concern for privilege with Jesus' abdication of privilege on the cross. Jesus' sacrifice of himself on the cross was an act of giving up his privilege for each of us. Jesus is the great example of one who gave of himself for those who had less. In Psalm 150, we have seen the dispelling of privilege for humans and the exaltation of God through praise. In the Synoptics, we see again the dispelling of privilege for humans, but this time in contrast to the sacrifice on the cross. Both undergird the biblical vision that God is supreme and loves sacrificially. Neither gives humans any privilege except to praise and serve God. The biblical vision is a leveling vision. It is a vision in which the world is full of variety, but in which none of the varieties is superior or inferior.

When Will the Kingdom Come?

Where in the world has the biblical vision been manifest? Is the biblical version any more successful than the political and social visions of human dreamers? When Christians search for a way to describe a world better than our present one, we often return to Revelation 21. And in many cases, the new heaven and new earth seem mostly like heaven into which the saved will be taken at the end of time. But Revelation scholar Rick Lowery sees the new heaven and the new earth a different way. They are the coming realm in which God is no longer separated from the earth, but present with us in it. Instead of dwelling in a temple, God is dwelling with the people. "The people are God's dwelling place . . . the new world is God's temple."

The new world in which we become a dwelling place for God is one in which all the fears, hatred, and racism of this world are left behind. Images of heaven, earth, city, and temple are blended into one and everything is described as new. But this is not just a world to be hoped for. This is a world that we, as Christians, can help build. We can open ourselves up to the indwelling of God. We can live in God's undeserved graciousness and start anew in a place where tears will be no more and all of God's people will live in peace. And the races will live together in harmony to make a beautiful new home for God.

Making a New World

Taking to heart Psalm 150, Christians can take a first step toward making a new world by giving up privileges in exchange for a vocation of praise. That is not a small step. Racial privilege of European Americans is part of the very fabric of North American experience. Few of us have any idea how often we invoke privileges or how often racism confronts people of color each day. As a parent of children of color, I am constantly reminded of how vulnerable my children are. Black teenagers in the wrong place at the wrong time suffer much more serious consequences than their white friends. Many of the boys at the high school want to be Mary's friends, but few are willing to date someone who is of mixed racial background. Neighbors still ask our children whether they are "confused" about their racial identity.

Christians are called to the task of ridding racism from our churches and our society in order to invite God to dwell with us. Furthermore, when we live without racism, we are examples to the world of what it truly means to be the interracial family of God. This is a painstaking and never-ending process. It is a process that can be quite discouraging and overwhelming, but at the same time, it is an act of justice that brings us joy by honoring the God who created us in all our variety. There is nothing so satisfying as living as God intended and being who God intended us to be.

I have seen this accomplished at times. Recently, I had a chance to tell the friends of my parents what wonderful examples and models they were for me. Nearly forty years ago, they adopted a child of another race. In the small, rural, Illinois town where they lived, adopting a black child was an act of true courage. I explained how much of an impression that action made on me as a teenager. Marian quietly thanked me for my kind words. When I told her I knew it could not have been easy, Marian got tears in her eyes. She said they were prepared for how the town would feel about what they had done, but they were not prepared for how the church reacted. She said, "They let us down." How sad! The church was the one place that should have been a safe place for this family. Still these people dared to live in a new heaven and earth as it should be, despite the old world around them.

A World Without Privilege

When we first decided to marry, our parents expressed great fears and reluctance. They were worried that the world would not be ready for an interracial couple, let alone an interracial family. They noticed all the stares from people in public that we seemed to overlook. Whether naive or courageous, we set out to make a marriage based on love that went beyond the boundaries of race.

Although we had racial differences, we had great similarities. We both grew up in Christian families of the same denomination. We both had middle-class economic backgrounds. We both attended our church college. I remember telling my parents that they could not be too unhappy as they were the ones who raised me to believe what I learned in church, for it was in church, not in society, that I sang songs about Jesus loving all the children of the world. It was in church where I learned that each person is loved by God. It was in church that Steve and I both found spiritual support.

But it has also been the church that at times has disappointed us. When Steve graduated from the seminary, he was looking forward to starting his ministry in a parish setting. In the end there were few opportunities for him. The predominantly white church was not ready for black ministers. Even though he had grown up in the church, he was still seen as an outsider. We were both thankful that he was ready to continue his studies at the doctoral level. It gave us a way to excuse the church. The very church that nurtured us and supported us had no room for us.

The church's hesitance to change is not the end of the story, however. As long as people continue to adopt children of other races into loving homes, cross race barriers in marriage, praise God instead of squabbling for places at God's side, and sacrifice their own privileges, the new heaven and new earth will establish a small foothold. These people are the pioneers of a new world. They are the dreamers who make an idea into reality. They are the ones who open the door to God and offer a dwelling place for God in the world.

For those who doubt the possibility of dreams becoming reality, there is a rich biblical record of such things. From an unlikely promise to Abraham and Sarah to an unlikely Savior and a small underground church movement in Palestine, the faith story is full of unreal realities. The monument over Martin Luther King, Jr.'s grave bears a verse from the Joseph story in Genesis, and on the very topic of dreaming. Joseph's brothers said to one another, "Behold, this dreamer cometh. Come now therefore, and let us slay him, . . . and we shall see what will become of his dreams" (37:19-20 KJV). What, indeed, will we do with this dream?

Discussion and Action

1. Read aloud Revelation 21:1-4, 22-25. Experiment as a group reading the scripture together from the same translation. How, if at all, does the way one reads it affect its meaning?

2. In a few minutes of silence, visualize what your life, your church, and the world would be like if there was less racism. How would things be different? Imagine the church as a true reflection of the interracial family of God. If you prefer, sketch your vision on paper or write down words and images that describe your vision. After the silent meditation, share your visions as a group,

3. Sing or read together "Beyond a dying sun." In what ways is the new world already upon us? How far have we come in bringing in a new world without racism? What is left to do to end racism?

4. How can you share with the congregation what you have learned about racism? Consider writing a litany of praise, a prayer of confession, or a statement of faith that can be used in worship.

5. Talk about how this series of lessons has affected your life. What have you learned? What was new? What was review? Prepare a list of things you plan to do in the next six months because of the things you have learned during these sessions.

6. Name some dreams in recent history that have come true. Who are some of the famous dreamers you admire? What realities do you dream about? How hopeful are you that your dreams will come true?

7. Pray as a group for forgiveness of the sins of prejudice and racism in each life and in the church. Ask God for courage and patience as you commit yourself to building the new Jerusalem. Pray for God's continued love for all as you bring this study to a close.

Suggestions for Sharing and Prayer

This material is designed for covenant groups that spend one hour sharing and praying together, followed by one hour of Bible study. The following suggestions will help relate the group's sharing and prayer time to their study of *Uncovering Racism*. Ideally, groups will use this opportunity to share with one another at an increasing depth as the weeks pass. Session-by-session ideas as well as several general resources for sharing and praying are provided in the following pages.

This section was written by René Calderon, a native of Ecuador. René is an ordained minister in the Church of the Brethren. Currently he teaches English as a second language in the schools of Grand Junction, Colorado.

1. Challenged by a Dream

❏ As a group, create a worship center. If you meet in the same place weekly, leave the worship center assembled for the next meeting. Put symbols of unity and harmony in the worship center, such as a unity candle, pictures cut from magazines, hands traced on paper and colored in many colors, or hymns in four-part harmony. Begin the sharing and prayer time by lighting a candle of illumination and praying silently for a few minutes for God's wisdom to come to you. This is a prerequisite for being open to God and to your neighbor. Wait until the end of your time together to extinguish the candle.

❏ As the four phrases of Psalm 139:23-24 are spoken, repeat them as a group. Pause after each phrase to meditate on the phrase.

❏ I became a Protestant in Ecuador, my homeland, at the age of 12. Automatically, I became part of the minority in religion and culture. When I was accepted at a college in the United States, I had a dream that I was going to be part of the Protestant majority. When I arrived in the U.S., to my surprise, I became part of the ethnic minority. In my life I have been in both positions, the one who discriminates as well as the one who is discriminated against. Share about a time you felt like a part of the majority and a time you felt part of the minority. How did your experiences compare? If you have a large group, share with one or two partners.

❏ People in the same racial group do not all think and act alike. Take a moment to think about how you personally are different from others in your race. Share your uniqueness with the group.

❏ Sing "Let my people go."

2. The Power That Oppresses

❏ Light the candle in the worship center. Listen as Psalm 4:2-3 is read three different times by three different people. This is a lament psalm. In quiet meditation think what it is about racism that you lament. After a moment of silence, offer a one-sentence lament about racism, if you're inclined.

❏ Everyone has power, even Christians. Listen as someone dramatically reads Exodus 14:21-22:

> Then Moses stretched out his hand over the sea. The LORD drove the sea back by a strong east wind all night, and turned the sea into dry land; and the waters were divided. The Israelites went into the sea on dry ground, the waters forming a wall for them on their right and on their left.

> As a group, focus on each individual in the group, naming the power you see in each person. Mention such powers as clear expression, insights, purchasing power, parental power, and the power of knowledge. Also say how this power can be used for good in each person.

❏ Share in a time of confession. Make your confessions silently to God, or aloud to God and the group. Confess racial stereotypes and prejudices you hold. Also name the power you have (financial, parental, managerial, political) to affect others based on your prejudices. Ask for the wisdom to use your power for good.

❏ Begin a timeline to track your experiences of race awareness. Each week you will plot an experience or event on the timeline that relates to the Bible study. This time, note the very first time you were conscious of races. Share your recollection with the group.

❏ Read the words to "Lift every voice and sing" and then sing it, or sing the South African hymn "Thuma Mina."

3. Misreading the Text

❏ Pass a Bible around the circle and add it to the worship center. Light the candle of illumination and listen as someone reads Genesis 9:18-27. Pray silently for the wisdom to understand scripture and to interpret it responsibly.

❏ If there is a person among you who has been the victim of racism, listen to his or her story. Feel free to ask questions, but do not make defensive responses. Close the story time by listening as someone reads Psalm 13.

❏ On an index card or piece of paper write "On the topic of racism, the Bible says . . . ." Then write the end of the sentence. Put the paper in a pile in the middle of the table and draw someone else's paper to read. Take turns reading the sentences aloud. How much agreement or disagreement is there about what the Bible says?

❏ Learn the song "Calvary" on page 105.

❏ Mark the approximate year on your timeline when you first heard that Genesis 9 was the justification of slavery.

4. The Subtlety of Racism

❑ Begin by lighting the candle of illumination. Take turns personally adding a symbol of subtle racism to the worship center. For example, a few coins might represent race discrimination in the economy, or a house key could represent race discrimination in real estate. Add symbols for subtle racism in churches, schools, or neighborhoods, or others that you think of. Tell what your symbol means as you place it in the worship center.

❑ My son went to Santiago, Chile, for his junior year. He happened to be walking in an area of Santiago where Chileans were demonstrating in remembrance of Pinochet's departure. Suddenly, he found himself in police custody; his belt and shoes were confiscated. Although my son informed them that he was an American, they did not believe him because he was dark skinned. One of his classmates had to go and get his passport before police would release him. What assumptions do people make when they see a person of another race— Asians, blacks, whites, Hispanics, American Indians? Spend a few moments in silent prayer confessing which assumptions you yourself make.

❑ One of the most impressive things about twelve-step programs is they require participants to be nonjudgmental. Share tips on how to curb yourself of making judgments about other people based on race or culture.

❑ Go to different places in the room or in the building to pray quietly. Pray Psalm 130, putting your name in the psalm whenever it say "I." When you come back together, talk about how reading your own name affected the meaning of the psalm for you.

❑ Sing "This little light of mine." Make up other verses about God's love for people of all colors and cultures.

❑ Put the approximate birth and death dates of a famous or well-respected person of color from your community or area on your timeline.

5. Racism and Hate Crimes

❑ Light the candle of illumination. Begin by praying for the
   victims of hate crimes and their perpetrators. In a period of
   silent meditation, call out the names of both and pause for
   prayer after each. In the worship center, place a cross to sym-
   bolize the fear and hatred that led to Jesus' execution.

❑ Use the words of a traditional spiritual to make a litany. Take
   turns reading an incident from the lists of hate crimes in Session 5. After the first one, respond by saying:

      We're gonna sit at the welcome table.

   After the second:
      *We're gonna sit at the welcome table one of these days.
      Hallelujah!*

   After the third:
      We're gonna sit at the welcome table one of these days.

   After the fourth:
      We're gonna sit at the welcome table . . .

   And so on.

❑ Learn to sing "When the storms of life are raging."

❑ On your timeline plot the date of a hate crime committed
   near you in this community or any other. Tell about the crime
   and how it affected you.

❑ Pass a photocopy of a U.S. map, or an actual map, around the
   room. With a marker, take turns marking some of the cities
   and towns that have experienced racial hate crimes. When
   the map has circulated around once or twice, place it in the
   middle of the group where everyone can see it. Offer sentence prayers for the end to hatred based on race.

6. The Costs and Profits of Racism

❑ Before lighting the candle of illumination, take time to check
   a label on your clothing, your wallet, your shoe, or some other

article you brought with you, to find where it was made. Write on an index card the name of the item, about how much it cost, and where it was made. Now light the candle. Read your card and place it in the worship center. Between each card, pray silently for the anonymous person who made the article and consider at what cost he or she made it. Do you imagine it was made at a sacrificial wage? in poor working conditions? where predominantly people of color live and work?

❑ If you could share with the world one poem, song, story, food, or tradition from your culture, what would it be? Share this with your covenant group. What new traditions did you learn from others? Commit yourself to trying someone else's tradition in worship, at a holiday, or at some other gathering.

❑ Use play money to meditate on what racism costs us in the church. Imagine you are the board of a church in which two congregations meet, one Hispanic and one white. Divide the money evenly between you. Each of you set aside money from your stash for two sets of Sunday school curriculum, one in Spanish and one in English. Set aside money for two pastors, two secretaries, and two organists. Put aside money for two evangelism programs or Bible school programs. How much did each of you spend? How much less would it cost to combine congregations and broaden the congregation's program? Share from experience which seems healthiest to you.

❑ Learn to sing "Guide my feet."

❑ Take turns reading the verses of Psalm 15 and Psalm 24:3-6, one verse per person. Pause between each verse to give a chance for silent meditation and self-reflection. According to these psalms, who is worthy to be a member of God's family? In reality, who is in God's family? Where do you fit in? Listen as those who wish share their reflections aloud.

❑ Plot on your timeline the approximate date you met your first friend from another race. Tell the group about your friend.

7. Our Struggle with Racism

❑ Add a hand mirror or a small, purse-size mirror to the worship center to represent looking inward. Light the candle and enter into a time of prayer and self-examination. Lay your prejudices before God, and name one prejudice aloud to the group if you wish. Close by reciting the Lord's Prayer.

❑ Find a partner to share ideas with. Together complete the sentence "Racism is a sin because . . . " on an index card. Come back together to share your completed sentences. Pile the sentences in the center. Draw cards until all are taken. Read them as a prayer, pausing between each one to say in unison, "Forgive us, Lord."

❑ Reflect privately, making a list of the privileges you enjoy in life, such as security, a good education, the protection of the law, and freedom to live where you want to live. After everyone has made a list, make one composite list on a large sheet of paper, eliminating duplicates. Take turns giving examples under each privilege of someone you know or have heard of who has been denied one of these privileges on account of race. Ponder whether you would be willing to forego any of these privileges at times so that someone else could benefit—a job offer, a scholarship, a low bid on a house.

❑ Take turns reading all of Psalm 51 (see p. 97). Then choose a verse of the psalm to write out on paper and illustrate or illuminate it by decorating capital letters or creating a decorative border. Keep the verse in your Bible, your journal, or in a file you use often. Or print your selection on a small card to carry in your wallet.

❑ Learn to sing "There is a balm in Gilead."

❑ Plot the approximate year or years on your timeline when you became aware of your own prejudices. Talk with the group about how you came to realize them.

8. Racism in the Church

❑ Together examine your denominational hymnal to see if it includes worship material from several cultures and languages. This is one indication of how people of different cultures contribute to your worship. Light the candle of illumination. Before adding the hymnal to the worship center, choose resources from it to sing or pray. If available, use a Native American resource, then a Hispanic resource, an African or African American resource, a European or European American resource, and an Asian resource. Read or sing a verse of each piece.

❑ Take a tour of the church building. If you're meeting in a home, take a "tour" through an illustrated Bible. As you are walking around individually, note objects or pieces of art that would have significance for people of various races. For instance, look for paintings of Jesus in the sanctuary, fellowship hall, and classrooms. What are Jesus' facial features and skin color in each? Do whites, Asians, African Americans, and American Indians in your congregation all find pictures of Jesus that look like them? Come back together and tell what you found. If you are meeting in a home, look at the artwork in a Bible. Does the art depict believers of many races?

❑ Learn to sing "I want Jesus to walk with me" on page 104.

❑ In groups of three or four, write a job description for a pastor. Share your job description with the larger group. Does race figure into any of the descriptions? Why? Prepare for a time of meditation. Take turns reading the stanzas of Psalm 41. With each new stanza, visualize a person of a different color reading from the pulpit. Close with prayers for a racially inclusive church.

❑ Plot three dates on your timeline: the year your denomination was integrated, the year your congregation was integrated, and the year of your first pastor of a different race (project a future date if this has not already happened).

9. Challenging Racism

❑ Light several candles from the main candle of illumination to represent a strong passion for justice. Stand along an imaginary continuum, one end of which is labeled "Highly motivated to combat racism," the other labeled "Not interested in being involved now." Position yourself at one end or the other or in between according to how strongly you feel. Share why you are standing where you are. Try another continuum. At one end are those who would like to work against all racism and at the other the people who are willing to confront racism in instances in which they are personally involved. Again, share your reasons for standing where you are.

❑ The story of Pentecost in Acts 2 describes a multicultural group. People present that day spoke many different languages, but they could understand each other. Invite the Holy Spirit into your presence during a period of silent prayer. Then take turns sharing what each of you thinks are the group's common understandings of racism. What are your common understandings of how to challenge racism? How difficult or easy is it to come to a common understanding?

❑ Listen as someone reads aloud Psalm 85. The psalmist asks three questions of God in the second stanza. Dwell in prayer on these questions to God, especially as they relate to the issue of racism. Devote several minutes to each question. After each question, share any clarity you received in prayer or contemplation on the matter.

❑ Learn to sing "De colores" or "Wade in the water."

❑ Psalm 85 says "righteousness and peace will kiss each other." Spend a few moments in silence. What images came to mind when you heard this sentence? Describe what it means to you.

❑ Mark the approximate date on your timeline of a time when you challenged a racist comment or deed. Tell the group about the situation.

10. Living Beyond Racism

❑ Begin by lighting the candle of illumination and placing a pair of eye glasses in the worship center to represent visions and dreams. Take turns giving your own "I have a dream" speech. Briefly tell others what your dream is for racial harmony. Close by offering sentence prayers for the fulfilling of the visions.

❑ Remember that God has removed barriers and made reconciliation possible. What barriers keep you from reaching across race lines to make your dream of racial equality a reality? Class barriers? Financial barriers? Theological barriers? Cultural barriers? Speak honestly among your covenant partners about your personal barriers. Then think together how each of you can bring the dream closer to reality by stepping over barriers. Can you, for instance, pledge to help each other keep commitments to stop telling racial jokes, work in pairs to relate to brothers and sisters of other races in other congregations, and take the initiative to bring people of all races together for worship or fellowship? Make a covenant with the group to get something done. Write up a contract. Hold each other accountable.

❑ Go as a group to a place where you can shout Psalm 150. If you wish, act out the psalm as someone shouts it out. While someone writes this psalm on poster board, leaving space at the bottom or around the border to paste pictures, cut pictures from news magazines of all kinds of people. Then put them in pairs, kings with peasants, billionaires with the poor, men with women, blacks with Asians, whites with Native Americans, the young with the elderly, and so on. Paste the pairs onto the poster to illustrate that no one is exalted above another except God. Mount the poster on a bulletin board where the congregation can see it and contemplate its message.

❑ Learn to sing "Beyond the dying sun."

❑ Look over the items in the worship center as a review of all you have considered in this study. Share what touched you most in the experience and how you might teach the children of the congregation about racism.

❑ Finish your timeline by posting the date in the future when you think the dream of racial equality will be realized in the church. Share with the group your hope or your despair about the future of racism.

General Sharing and Prayer Resources

Forming a Covenant Group

Covenant-making is significant throughout the biblical story. God made covenants with Noah, Abraham, and Moses. Jeremiah speaks about God making a covenant with the people, "written on the heart." In the New Testament, Jesus is identified as the mediator of the new covenant, and the early believers lived out of covenant relationships. Throughout history people have lived in covenant relationship with God and within community.

Christians today also covenant with God and make commitments to each other. Such covenants help believers live out their faith. God's empowerment comes to them as they gather in covenant communities to pray and study, share and receive, reflect and act.

People of the Covenant is a program that is anchored in this covenantal history of God's people. It is a network of covenantal relationships. Denominations, districts or regions, congregations, small groups, and individuals all make covenants. Covenant group members commit themselves to the mission statement, seeking to become more . . .

—biblically informed so they better understand the revelation of God;

—globally aware so they know themselves to be better connected with all of God's world;

—relationally sensitive to God, self, and others.

The Burlap Cross Symbol

The imperfections of the burlap cross, its rough texture and unrefined fabric, the interweaving of threads, the uniqueness of each strand, are elements that are present within the covenant group. The people in the groups are imperfect, unpolished, interrelated with each other, yet still unique beings.

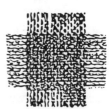

The shape that this collection of imperfect threads creates is the cross, symbolizing for all Christians the resurrection and presence of Christ our Savior. A covenant group is something akin to this burlap cross. It unites common, ordinary people and sends them out again in all directions to be in the world.

A Litany of Commitment

All: *We are a people of the covenant; out of our commitment to Christ, we seek to become:*

Group 1: more biblically informed so we understand better God's revelation;

Group 2: more globally aware so we know ourselves connected with all of God's people;

Group 1: more relationally sensitive to God, self, and others.

All: *We are a people of the covenant; we promise:*

Group 2: to seek ways of living out and sharing our faith;

Group 1: to participate actively in congregational life;

Group 2: to be open to the leading of the Spirit in our lives.

All: *We are a people of the covenant; we commit ourselves:*

Group 1: to attend each group meeting, so far as possible;

Group 2: to prepare through Bible study, prayer, and action;

Group 1: to share thoughts and feelings, as appropriate;

Group 2: to encourage each other on our faith journeys.

All: *We are a people of the covenant.*

A Litany on Reconciliation

Leader: If anyone is in Christ, there is a new creation;
          everything old has passed away;
          see, everything has become new!

All: *All this is from God,*
          who reconciled us to himself through Christ,
          and has given us the ministry of reconciliation;
          that is, in Christ God was reconciling the world to
              himself,
          not counting their trespasses against them,
          and entrusting the message of reconciliation to us.

Leader: So we are ambassadors for Christ,
          since God is making his appeal through us;
          we entreat you on behalf of Christ, be reconciled to
              God.

All: *For our sake he made him to be sin who knew no sin,*
          so that in him we might become the righteousness of
              God.

                                        —2 Corinthians 5:17-21

An Act of Commitment

One: God so loved the world that an only Son was given.

Everyone: He came as light to the darkness within us, as life to
          our hunger and thirst for meaning, as a way for our
          confusion and lostness.

One: He came as one in whom we can all enjoy the comfort
          and joy of being one.

Everyone: The reality of oneness in Christ is a truth I deeply de-
          sire to own and genuinely want to learn to live. When
          I am tempted to be prejudiced against another, I will
          remember, "I am baptized." When I hate or abhor an-
          other, I will say to myself, "I am baptized." When I
          mistreat or neglect or purposefully turn away from one
          for whom Christ died, I will silently say, "I am bap-
          tized." No longer can I say, "I love God," and dislike

> *or mistreat a brother or sister. I desire to honor my baptism; to recommit myself; to begin, in this life, to live the vision of every nation and all tribes and all peoples, one in Christ, standing in worship and praise before the throne of God.*

Earle W. Fike, Jr. Racism and the Church, Vol. 2.
Church of the Brethren General Board, 1995

Psalm 51

[1] Have mercy on me, O God, according to your steadfast love; according to your abundant mercy blot out my transgressions.

[2] Wash me thoroughly from my iniquity, and cleanse me from my sin.

[3] For I know my transgressions, and my sin is ever before me.

[4] Against you, you alone, have I sinned, and done what is evil in your sight, so that you are justified in your sentence and blameless when you pass judgment.

[5] Indeed, I was born guilty, a sinner when my mother conceived me.

[6] You desire truth in the inward being; therefore teach me wisdom in my secret heart.

[7] Purge me with hyssop, and I shall be clean; wash me, and I shall be whiter than snow.

[8] Let me hear joy and gladness; let the bones that you have crushed rejoice.

[9] Hide your face from my sins, and blot out all my iniquities.

[10] Create in me a clean heart, O God, and put a new and right spirit within me.

[11] Do not cast me away from your presence, and do not take your holy spirit from me.

[12] Restore to me the joy of your salvation, and sustain in me a willing spirit.

¹³ Then I will teach transgressors your ways, and sinners will return to you.

¹⁴ Deliver me from bloodshed, O God, O God of my salvation, and my tongue will sing aloud of your deliverance.

¹⁵ O Lord, open my lips, and my mouth will declare your praise.

¹⁶ For you have no delight in sacrifice; if I were to give a burnt offering, you would not be pleased.

¹⁷ The sacrifice acceptable to God is a broken spirit; a broken and contrite heart, O God, you will not despise.

¹⁸ Do good to Zion in your good pleasure; rebuild the walls of Jerusalem,

¹⁹ then you will delight in right sacrifices, in burnt offerings and whole burnt offerings; then bulls will be offered on your altar.

Timeline
B.C.E.— Before the Common Era.
> In biblical studies it has been noted that B.C., a christocentric way of seeing time, is inappropriate for a Bible that includes Jews as well as Christians. Hence the abbreviation B.C.E.

C.E.—Common Era

1500 B.C.E.	**Wanderings as Migrant Workers and Herders**
	Genesis tells us that Abram is a wealthy herder. However, he is not native to the land of Canaan. As a non-native he has less status and power. But we should notice the text's assumption of cultural superiority described in the stories of Hagar and later in the Joseph narratives.
1300–1200 B.C.E.	**Slavery in Egypt**
	According to Genesis Joseph rose to a high rank in the Egyptian government. His family came to Egypt as the result of a drought,

in an attempt to find food. But in these stories it is clear that Joseph is the consistent
outsider. When he dies and the Egyptian
ruler no longer regards Joseph's people,
they become slaves. The Egyptians assume
a cultural superiority, which the Hebrews
dispute with stories like Exodus 1–2.

1200–1100 B.C.E. **Migrant Workers and Herders**
As refugees led by Moses, the Hebrews
wander in the desert after fleeing Egypt.
They are mobile like Abraham, but without
his wealth and status. They are the poor
migrant homeless, working at times, idle
at others.

1100–1000 B.C.E. **Conquest of the Land of Canaan**
Now with a perceived mandate from God,
the Hebrews try to extinguish the Canaanite
presence in the region. They have only limited success (see Judges 1). Nonetheless,
the Hebrews have a land in which they can
claim cultural superiority and make it stick
by rule of force.

1000 B.C.E. **United Monarchy**
The monarchy, first under Saul and later
David, becomes one of the prime institutions for maintaining cultural superiority,
for the Philistine threat is both military and
cultural. The matter of culture and faith traditions will continue to be an issue for the
monarchy. Also in this period, the tribalism that existed in each of the previous eras
now has to accommodate the superiority of
the monarchy. With one people under one
king, tribalism must be set aside. The mon-

archy will continue to struggle with this conflict, though admittedly, cultural threats are less significant in this era.

920 B.C.E.   **Divided Monarchy**
During the Divided Monarchy the tribal power reasserts itself, resulting in the break-up of the United Monarchy. The threat from other cultures becomes substantially more profound with incursions from Egypt, Damascus, Assyria (who will destroy the North Kingdom in 722), and ultimately from Babylonia. The Babylonians eventually destroy Jerusalem in 587. During this period the Hebrews are able to maintain their cultural heritage but the press of more dominant cultures is felt.

722 B.C.E.   **Fall of the Northern Kingdom**
After an attempt to regain cultural and political autonomy, the Assyrians destroy the Syrians (Damascus) in 734 and put a puppet on the throne in Samaria, capital of the Israelites' Northern Kingdom. But when Samaria tries to break away a decade later, the city of Samaria is destroyed and the Assyrian re-population program brings in immigrants who are called Samaritans. From that time forward the earlier tribal differences are accentuated. We see much anti-Samaritan sentiment in the New Testament.

587 B.C.E.   **Colony of Babylon**
The community strives to retain its culture in a foreign land without bringing on the wrath of the dominant Babylonian culture.

539 B.C.E.   **Colony of Persia**
The Persians provide a more subtle cultural
imperialism. On the face of it, they support
Ezra and Nehemiah in their attempts to re-
constitute the religious traditions of the
Hebrews, who are increasingly called
Judeans, from which the word *Jew* will
come. Nonetheless, one can note similarities between Persian theological ideas and
some of the biblical material from this age,
suggesting more than a hands-off policy
toward Judah.

333 B.C.E.   **Colony of Greece and Its Later Satellites**
Alexander the Great conquers the region at
the Battle of Issus (333). Alexander believes
the entire world should express Greek culture. He is an astute politician and is able
to blend native and Greek traditions. When
he dies (300), the region falls to his Egyptian general from Syria, who does not have
his skills of blending cultures.

167–164 B.C.E.   **Maccabean Revolt**
This is a fight for freedom of religious and
cultural expression. Despite strong Jewish
resistance to Syrian occupation, a revolt
does not win complete freedom from cultural dominance. The leader is a Jewish
priest, Judas Maccabeus.

63 B.C.E.   **Colony of Rome**
During this time tribes continue as a force,
but now religious parties, such as the
Sadducees and the Pharisees, gain
strength and support different factions of
the ruling family. The Romans are brought

in as allies by the Sadducees. The Romans then annex the region.

4–33 C.E   **Jesus' Life and Ministry**
During this period Jesus ministers to the Jews, though he has contact with people outside that group. At this point the Jesus movement is a Jewish sub-group.

10–62 C.E.   **Paul**
Paul brings his ministry to both Jews and Gentiles. His focus on Gentiles causes significant conflict for the Jews, because they are exposed to a cultural diversity they had not had before.

66–70 C.E.   **First Jewish Revolt**
The Jewish revolt against Rome is an attempt for independence. The same issues are present that drove the Maccabean revolt.

135 C.E.   **Second Jewish Revolt**
This revolt is often named for its leader *bar Cochba* (son of the star), who thought that God would bring about the victory after the righteous began to rebel against the pagan Romans. However, Jerusalem is razed and Judaism becomes an outlawed religion by the Romans.

Wade in the water

Wade in the wa - ter, wade in the wa - ter, chil - dren,

wade in the wa - ter. God's gon-na trou-ble the wa - ter.

Leader   All

1 See those peo - ple dressed in white, God's gon - na trou - ble the

Leader

wa - ter. They must be the chil-dren of the Is - rael - ites.

All   D.C.

God's gon - na trou - ble the wa - ter.

2 See those people dressed in black ...   They come a long way and they ain't turning back.
3 See those people dressed in blue ...   They look like my people coming through.
4 See those people dressed in red ...   They must be the children that Moses led.
5 Some say Peter, some say Paul ...   There ain't but one God made them all.

Text: African American spiritual
Music: African American spiritual

I want Jesus to walk with me

```
1      I  want  Je - sus      to  walk with   me.
2      In  my   tri - als,    Lord, walk with  me.
3 When I'm in  trou - ble,    Lord, walk with  me.
```

```
       I  want  Je - sus      to  walk  with   me.
       In  my   tri - als,    Lord, walk  with  me.
  When I'm in  trou - ble,    Lord, walk  with  me.
```

```
       All  a - long  my      pil - grim  jour - ney,
       When my  heart  is      al - most  break - ing,
       When my  head   is      bowed  in   sor - row,
```

```
  Lord,  I want  Je - sus     to  walk with   me.
  Lord,  I want  Je - sus     to  walk with   me.
  Lord,  I want  Je - sus     to  walk with   me.
```

Text: African American spiritual
Music: African American spiritual

Calvary

Cal - va - ry, Cal - va - ry, Cal - va -

ry, Cal - va - ry, Cal - va - ry, Cal - va -

ry, sure - ly he died on Cal - va - ry.

1 Ev - 'ry time I think a-bout Je - sus, ev - 'ry time I
2 Don't you hear the ham - mer ring-ing? Don't you hear the
3 Don't you hear him call-ing his Fa - ther? Don't you hear him
4 Don't you hear him say, "It is fin-ished"? Don't you hear him
5 Je - sus fur-nished my sal - va - tion. Je - sus fur-nished
6 Sin - ner, do you love my Je - sus? Sin - ner, do you

1 think a-bout Je - sus, ev - 'ry time I think a-bout Je - sus,
2 ham - mer ring-ing? Don't you hear the ham - mer ring-ing?
3 call-ing his Fa - ther? Don't you hear him call-ing his Fa - ther?
4 say, "It is fin-ished"? Don't you hear him say "It is fin-ished"?
5 my sal - va - tion. Je - sus fur-nished my sal - va - tion.
6 love my Je - sus? Sin - ner, do you love my Je - sus?

Sure - ly he died on Cal - va - ry.

Text: African American spiritual
Music: African American spiritual

Other Covenant Bible Studies

To place an order, call Brethren Press toll-free Monday through Friday, 8 A.M. to 4 P.M., at **800-441-3712**, or fax an order to **800-667-8188** twenty-four hours a day. Shipping and handling will be added to each order. For a full description of each title, ask for a free catalog of these and other Brethren Press titles.

Visa and MasterCard accepted. Prices subject to change.

Brethren Press® • *faithQuest*® • 1451 Dundee Ave., Elgin, IL 60120-1694
800-441-3712 (orders) • 800-667-8188